A
Guide to
Tracing Your Dublin Ancestors

James G. Ryan

Brian Smith

Flyleaf
Press

A division of Ancestor Network

First published in 1988
Second Edition 1998
Third Edition 2009
Fourth Edition 2017

Flyleaf Press
4 Spencer Villas
Glenageary
Co. Dublin, Ireland
www.flyleaf.ie

© 2017 Flyleaf Press

ISBN 978-1-907990-31-1

The information in this book is subject to change without notice.

Cover Illustration:

Custom House, Dublin
from
Ireland: Its Scenery, Character, etc. (Vol.II)
by
Mr. and Mrs. S.C. Hall
(London 1842)

Layout:
Brian Smith

929.1072

Items should be returned on or before the last date shown below. Items not already requested by other borrowers may be renewed in person, in writing or by telephone. To renew, please quote the number on the barcode label. To renew online a PIN is required. ᴐrs This can be requested at your local library.
Renew online @ **www.dublincitypubliclibraries.ie**
Fines charged for overdue items will include postage incurred in recovery. Damage to or loss of items will be charged to the borrower.

Leabharlanna Poiblí Chathair Bhaile Átha Cliath
Dublin City Public Libraries

Dublin City
Baile Átha Cliath

Date Due	Date Due	Date Due
	1 8 DEC 2017	

Contents

Abbreviations Used

Anal Hib	Analecta Hibernica (Journal)
aka	also known as
Arch.	Archaeological
b.	birth/born
bapt.	Baptism
BL	British Library
c.	circa
Co.	County
CoI	Church of Ireland
d.	death/died
ed.	editor/edited (by)
DCLA	Dublin City Library and Archive
DCPL	Dublin City Public Libraries
DHG	Dublin Heritage Group
DKPRI	(Reports of the) Deputy Keeper of Public Records of Ireland
DLBHS	Dun Laoghaire Borough Historical Society
DLGS	Dun Laoghaire Genealogical Society
DLHC	Dun Laoghaire Heritage Centre
DU	Dublin (Diocese)
Dublin Hist. Rec.	Dublin Historical Record
FHS	Family History Society
GO	Genealogical Office
GRO	General Register Office
GSI	Genealogical Society of Ireland
Hist.	Historical
IGP	Irish Genealogical Project
IGRS	Irish Genealogical Research Society
IMA Par. Reg. Sect.	Irish Memorials Association Parish Register Section
Ir. Anc.	Irish Ancestor
Ir. Gen.	Irish Genealogist
J. or Jnl.	Journal
JAPMD	Journal of Association for the Preservation of Memorials of the Dead

J. Gen. Soc. I.	Journal of Genealogical Society of Ireland
J. KAHS.	Journal of the Kildare Archaeological and Historical Society
LC	Local Custody
LDS	Latter Day Saints (Family History Centre)
Lib.	Library
m. or marr.	marriage/married
MEMS: Dublin	Memorials of the Dead -Dublin City & County
mf.	microfilm
Ms/Mss	Manuscript/s
NAI	National Archives of Ireland (formerly PRO)
n.d.	not dated
NLI	National Library of Ireland
OP	Official Papers
p./pp.	page/pages
PHSI	Presbyterian Historical Society of Ireland
Pos.	Positive
PRO	Public Record Office (now National Archives of Ireland)
PRONI	Public Record Office of Northern Ireland
Pub.	published/publisher
RC	Roman Catholic
RCB(L)	Representative Church Body (Library)
Rept.	Report
RIA	Royal Irish Academy
RIC	Royal Irish Constabulary
RSAI	Royal Society of Antiquarians in Ireland (J. of)
SHS	Swords Historical Society Ltd.
SLC	Family History Library, Salt Lake City (and branches)
Soc.	Society
SPO	State Paper Office
TCD	Trinity College Dublin
UCD	University College Dublin

Provincial Boundaries

Chapter 1   Introduction

Dublin's history goes back as far as AD. 140 when Ptolemy noted a settlement on this site. The city has had a long history as a Norse Viking settlement, a Gaelic city, a Norman city, as the centre of colonial English Administration of Ireland, as the centre of Irish rebellion early in the 20th century and currently as the capital of modern Ireland.

Since Dublin's establishment, Dubliners have grown considerably in number and eminence. The earliest city population estimate is 1644 when 8,000 people were recorded. By 1682 it had risen to 60,000; by 1728 it was 146,000; by 1800 it was 170,000; and by 1841 the city had over 230,000 inhabitants. During the Great Famine of 1845-47 the population greatly expanded due to migration of people from other badly affected parts of the country. Just before the famine, in 1841, the population of Dublin city and county was 372,000. By 1851 it had grown to 405,000. The population of the county grew only slowly during the remainder of the century but has grown rapidly since the foundation of the Irish state in 1921. The population of Dublin county and city in 2016 was 1.273 Million.

It is reasonable to suggest that modern Dubliners include descendants of the original native Dubliners. They also include descendants of the later arrivals, i.e. the Norse, Norman, English, Huguenot, Jewish and other groups. The predominant population group, however, is Irish people from other parts of the country.

Although descendants of Norsemen undoubtedly remain in much of the county, particularly north of the city, their influence is not obvious in Dublin family names because they did not use hereditary surnames or family names. Anglo-Norman families who settled in the county include Baggot, Sarsfield, Luttrell, Delahyde, Talbot, Barnewall, St. Lawrence, Cruise, Archbold, and Segrave.

Tracing Dublin Families

This book is intended to assist those who wish to establish their links with those Dubliners who defended, ran and worked the city over the ages; who inspired its writers, artist and leaders, built its great buildings and otherwise contributed to the city's existence and fame.

Tracing a family history normally requires the researcher to consult many different historical sources, in some (or hopefully all) of which details of the family may be found. Sufficient details, when pieced together, can form a comprehensive picture of a family's existence. Although Irish sources for family history are sparse relative to some other European countries, Dublin has arguably the best variety of family history resources in Ireland. However, like all cities, individual families can be hard to find within this variety.

This book outlines the range of different types of records available to the Dublin family researcher. The nature, time-frames and locations of the available sources is described in the following chapters. Descriptions of available sources are arranged by chapter according to source type i.e. civil registration, church records, censuses, census substitutes, newspapers, directories etc.

For optimal use of these records, it is important to understand the system of administrative divisions used in Ireland. These divisions or areas are described in Chapter 2. They are vital in determining an ancestor's address or location. Many, if not most sources are arranged according to such divisions, and an understanding of the different elements of an ancestors address is therefore important.

The abbreviations used are explained on pages 6 to 7 and the contact details for the organisations and archives cited are in Chapter 13. Most publications cited are to be found in major genealogical libraries and increasingly on-line.

Chapter 2   Administrative Divisions

An ancestor's address is a basic element of identity as well as being an essential step in obtaining further information. To understand the make-up of addresses cited in different records, it is necessary to know about the various administrative areas used. Dublin was, and is, divided into different units or divisions for the purposes of both Civil and Ecclesiastical administration. These divisions are an important factor in locating the records mentioned throughout this book. They are as follows:

Civil Divisions:

Townland
The townland is the smallest civil division within a county. Although they exist in urban areas, they are not generally used as street addresses are more convenient. They are effectively only used in rural areas. The townland is an ancient division of land which is highly variable in size, and may vary from less than 10 acres to several thousand. It is the most specific part of an ancestor's address in rural areas.

Civil Parish
The civil parish is the land division which most commonly occurs in Irish records. There are 83 civil parishes in County Dublin, each is formed of many townlands or city areas. Dublin City is divided into 23 civil parishes. It should be noted that some civil parishes cross barony and county boundaries. In some cases also, civil parishes are divided into unconnected parts. See maps between pages 18 and 21.

Barony
Civil parishes are grouped into Baronies. This division is generally based on the ancient 'tuath' or territory of an Irish clan. There are 9 baronies in Co. Dublin but they are not widely used in records. See maps between pages 18 and 21.

Poor Law Union

These were established under the Poor Law Act of 1838 for use in the administration of distress relief and the upkeep of the poor and destitute. They are unrelated to any other division and do not adhere to county and barony borders. Each is based around (and named from) a major town in which was based the workhouse and other administrative functions of the Poor Law. The Poor Law Union (PLU) later came to be used as the area, or district, in which Civil Registration of births, marriages and deaths was conducted. There are 7 PLUs in Dublin.

The **District Electoral Division** (DED) is a sub-division of the Poor Law union, in which census information was compiled and in which the census returns are also arranged. They were also used for the elections of local and national representatives.

Borough. A town, or part of a city, with a Corporation and/or which had the right to elect a Member to the British Parliament at Westminster.

Ward. A division of a municipal borough (q.v.) for the purpose of electing councillors, or of a civil parish for the purpose of electing guardians.

Ecclesiastical Divisions:

Church of Ireland Parish

The ecclesiastical divisions used by the Church of Ireland (CoI) had a specific significance for record purposes as the CoI was also the 'Established' or State church. In this capacity it once performed several functions now performed by the State. These include Probate (proving of wills), and granting of marriage and other forms of licence. Church of Ireland divisions therefore have a relevance when researching certain record types. Note that, while generally conforming to the civil parish boundaries, some CoI churches served several civil parishes.

Catholic Church Parish

Catholic Church parish boundaries rarely conform to those of the Civil parish, even though they may have the same name as the civil parish in which they are located. They are often of ancient origin, and generally larger in size than Church of Ireland parishes.

Useful Guides to Administrative Divisions:

To establish the divisions which make up an ancestor's 'genealogical address' the following references are useful:

There are several useful on-line Townland mapping guides: The government agency with responsibility is the Ordnance Survey Office. Their site http://maps.osi.ie/publicviewer has an excellent system which overlays maps of different vintages and scales on any site. Further background is also available at http://wiki.openstreetmap.org/wiki/Ireland/Mapping_Townlands To find the location of a townland try www.thecore.com/seanruad/

1851 Townland Index of Ireland
This provides a full alphabetic listing of all of the Townlands, Towns, Civil Parishes and Baronies of Ireland giving their relative location, area and map reference. For each townland the relevant County, Barony, Civil Parish and Poor Law Union is provided. This listing was derived from the areas used by officials compiling the 1851 Census. It was originally published by Thom's as *'An Index to the Townlands and Towns, Parishes and Baronies of Ireland'*. It has been republished by the Genealogical Publishing Co., Baltimore, US and is widely available in libraries. It is available on-line at www.irishancestors.ie/?page_id=5392. Similar volumes were compiled for the Censuses of 1841, 1861, 1871 etc. and may be found in many libraries. The spelling and occurrence of some townlands varied between censuses and it may occasionally be useful to consult some of these. See also - https://www.townlands.ie/

Townlands in Poor Law Unions
This publication is divided by Poor Law Union (PLU), each of which is arranged by District Electoral Division (DED) and then Civil Parish. It is very useful for indentifying neighbouring townlands in a Civil Parish. Complied by George B. Handran and published by Higginson (USA 1997). See also - https://www.townlands.ie/

Lewis's Topographical Dictionary of Ireland
Contains an alphabetically arranged account of all parishes, towns and many villages, and a map of each county. For each it provides a brief history, an account of social and economic conditions, and the names of major landowners. First published in 1837, it has been republished in several editions and is widely available. See p.14. It is available on-line at www.askaboutireland.ie/reading-room/digital-book-collection.

LUCAN, a post-town and parish, in the barony of NEWCASTLE, county of DUBLIN, and province of LEINSTER, 7 miles (W.) from Dublin, on the mail road to Galway and Sligo; containing 1755 inhabitants, of which number, 1229 are in the town. After the English settlement it appears to have been granted to Richard de Peche, one of the earliest English adventurers, and in 1220 was the property of Waryn de Peche, who founded the monastery of St. Catherine, near Leixlip. In the reign of Rich. II. it was in the possession of the Rokeby family, and in the 16th century it belonged to the Sarsfield family, of whom William, one of the ablest generals in the service of Jas. II., was by that monarch, after his abdication, created Earl of Lucan, from whom it descended by marriage to the ancestor of Col. G. Vesey, its late proprietor. The town is beautifully situated in a fertile vale on the eastern bank of the river Liffey, over which is a handsome stone bridge of one arch, built in 1794, and ornamented with balustrades of cast iron from the Phœnix iron-works, near Dublin. At the other side of the bridge, on the eastern bank of the river, is the picturesque glebe of the incumbent, the Rev. H. E. Prior. The total number of houses is 187, most of which are well built, and many of them are fitted up as lodging-houses for the reception of visiters, who, during the summer season, resort to this place to drink the waters, which are found efficacious in scorbutic, bilious, and rheumatic affections. A handsome Spa-house has been erected, consisting of a centre and two wings, in one of which is an assembly-room, 62 feet long and 22 feet wide, in which concerts and balls are given; the house affords excellent accommodation for families. The mineral spring, from its having a higher temperature than others in the neighbourhood, is called the " Boiling Spring;" the water, on an analysis made in 1822, was found to contain, in two gallons, 70 grains of crystallised carbonate of soda, 20 of carbonate of lime, $1\frac{1}{2}$ of carbonate of magnesia, 2 of silex, $6\frac{1}{2}$ of muriate of soda, and 14 of sulphur. The scenery of the neighbourhood is beautifully diversified, and its short distance from the metropolis renders the town a place of fashionable resort and of pleasant occasional residence. A

A description of Lucan from
'Lewis's Topigraphical Dictionary of Ireland' (1837)
see p.13

Parliamentary Gazetteer of Ireland (1844/5)

This is similar to Lewis's Topographical Dictionary in content and arrangement. Published in three volumes-Vol. I A-C (1845); Vol. II (D-M) (1845); Vol. III (N-Z) + index (1846). NLI Ir. 9141 p30

Ordnance Survey Field Name Books

The Ordnance Survey (OS) (www.osi.ie) is Ireland's official State map-maker. The Field Name Books are the notebooks used by the surveyors compiling the first OS maps of Ireland. They are arranged by civil parish, and list each townland alphabetically. Although varying slightly between areas, the following details are usually included:

Townland name in Irish and English; Derivation of the name; Location within the parish; Proprietor's name; and other comments (See illustration below).

The original transcripts are on microfilm in the NLI, the typescripts in hard copy are also held there. The reference numbers are as follows:

Aderrig - Coolock	Ir 92942 o3 Book 47
Donabate - Kiltiernan	Ir 92942 o3 Book 48
Killossery - Old Connaught	Ir 92942 o3 Book 49
Palmerstown - Whitechurch	Ir 92942 o3 Book 50
Dublin City Parishes	Ir 92942 o3 Book 51

Microfilms of these are in NLI Pos.1398 and 1406. The following two pages list the Civil Parishes of Dublin County, and the alternate names occasionally found. They also show the years in which Griffith's Valuation (see p.122) and the Tithe Applotment surveys were conducted, and the reference number for the Civil Parish map on page 19. A similar list for the City Parishes would serve no useful purpose.

The Field name books are also available in pdf format through a search facility on http://www.askaboutireland.ie/griffith-valuation/index. xml?action=nblSearch

---

```
Cabinteely Village              -- Bdy. Sr. Sk. Map              19

              Cabán t-Síle, Sheela's Cabin, or Celia's Cabin.
       Cabinteely
       Cabinteely                     -- Inhabitants
       Cabinteely                     -- J. Cooke, Cabinteely
              At the junction of Cabinteely, Kilbogget, Loughlins-
       town Tnldx and Brennanstown Tnlds.

              A clean little village on the road from Dublin to
       Bray.   It is composed of 3 or 4 public Houses, A Baker's
       & Butcher's shop.   A fine chapel has been lately erected
       here, for which see Description of Kill.
```

The entry for Cabinteely from the 'Ordnance Survey Field Name Books'

Dublin County Civil Parishes A - Z

Map Ref	Civil Parish (Barony)	Griffith Valuation	Tithe	Alternate name forms
49	Aderrig	1851	1831	
39.	Artane	1848	n/a	(see Finglas), Artaine
5.	Baldongan	1852	1833	Baldungan
36.	Baldoyle	1848	n/a	-
34.	Balgriffin	1848	1834	
14.	Ballyboghil	1848	1833	Ballyboghill
59.	Ballyfermot	1850	1828	-
10.	Ballymadun	1848	1833	Ballymodun
2.	Balrothery	1852	1833	-
1.	Balscadden	1852	1834	-
71.	Booterstown	1849	1826	-
26.	Castleknock	1849	1828	-
27.	Chapelizod	1849	1834	-
23.	Cloghran (Castleknock)	1849	n/a	
31.	Cloghran (Coolock)	1848	1827	Cloghran/Swords
58.	Clondalkin	1850	1827/34	-
12.	Clonmethan	1848	1833	-
25.	Clonsilla	1849	1828	Clonsillagh
46.	Clontarf	1848	1829	-
38.	Clonturk	1848	n/a	Drumcondra
35.	Coolock	1848	1823	-
66.	Cruagh	1850	1833	Crevagh
62.	Crumlin	1850	1827	Cromlin
78.	Dalkey	1849	1826/46	-
17.	Donabate	1848	1830	Donaghbate
68.	Donnybrook	1849/50	1824	-
61.	Drimnagh	1850	1827	Drimna
50.	Esker	1850/51	1825	-
24.	Finglas	1848/49	1828	-
7.	Garristown	1848	1833	-
37.	Glasnevin	1848	1828	-
8.	Grallagh	1848	1833	-
43.	Grangegorman	1848	1833	-

Dublin County Civil Parishes A - Z contd.

Map Ref	Civil Parish (Barony)	Griffith Valuation	Tithe	Alternate name forms
9.	Hollywood	1848	1833	-
3.	Holmpatrick	1852	n/a	Skerries
42.	Howth	1848	n/a	-
41.	Kilbarrack	1848	n/a	-
53.	Kilbride	1851	n/a	-
79.	Kilgobbin	1849	1828	Kilgobban
77.	Kill	1849	1826 & 46	Kill of the Grange
20.	Killeek	1848	n/a	Killaugh
45.	Killester	1848	1833	-
80.	Killiney	1849	1826	-
15.	Killossery	1848	1824	-
51.	Kilmactalway	1851	1828	-
73.	Kilmacud	1849	1826	-
52.	Kilmahuddrick	1851	1834	-
32.	Kilsaley	1848	1824	Kinsaley or Kinsealy
19.	Kilsallaghan	1848	1821	-
81.	Kiltiernan	1849	1833	-
47.	Leixlip	1851	1825	-
48.	Lucan	1851	n/a	- (see Esker)
4.	Lusk	1852	1833	-
28.	Malahide	1848	n/a	-
75.	Monkstown	1849	1826	-
22.	Mulhuddart	1849	1828	Mulhuddert Mullahitart
6.	Naul	1848	1835	-
54.	Newcastle	1851	1827	Newcastle-juxta- Lyons
83.	Old Connaught	1849	1826	Old Conna or Connagh
11.	Palmerston (Balrothery W)	1848	1833	-
57.	Palmerstown (Uppercross)	1850	1828	-
33.	Portmarnock	1848	1832	Port St. Marnock
18.	Portraine	1848	1834	Portrane, Portrahan
40.	Raheny	1848	1830	-
55.	Rathcoole	1851	1825	-

Dublin County Civil Parishes A - Z contd.

Map Ref	Civil Parish (Barony)	Griffith Valuation	Tithe	Alternate name forms
69.	Rathfarnham	1849/50	1825	-
82	Rathmichael	1849	1826	-
56.	Saggart	1851	1831	Tassagart
30.	Santry	1848	1830	Santreff
63.	St. Catherine	1850	1830	-
44.	St. George	1848	1833	(see also Glasnevin)
60.	St. James'	1849/50	1829	-
29.	St. Margaret	1848	n/a	(see also Finglas)
67.	St. Mark	1849	n/a	-
64.	St. Peter	1849/50	1833	-
3.	Skerries			see Holmpatrick
74.	Stillorgan	1849	1827	-
16.	Swords	1848	1830	-
65.	Tallaght	1850	1826	-
70.	Taney	1849	1824	Tawney
76.	Tully	1849	1826/46	Tullow or Bullock
21.	Ward	1849	n/a	(see also Finglas)
13.	Westpalstown	1852	1833	-
72.	Whitechurch	1849	1832	-

Baronies of Dublin
1. Balrothery East
2. Balrothery West
3. Nethercross
4. Castleknock
5. Coolock
6. Newcastle
7. Uppercross
8. Dublin
9. Rathdown

Civil Parishes of Dublin - see p.20 for map index

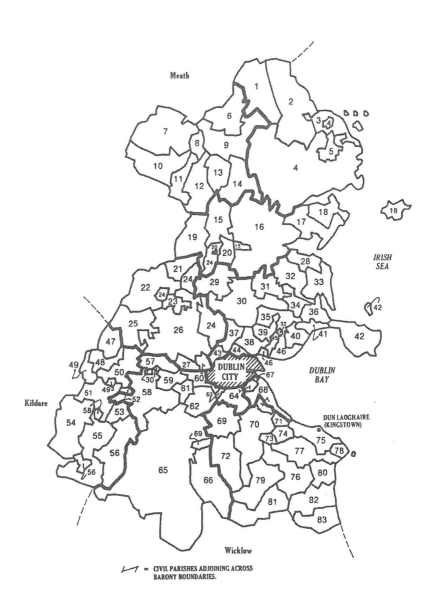

Meath

Kildare

IRISH
SEA

DUBLIN
BAY

DUBLIN
CITY

DUN LAOGHAIRE
(KINGSTOWN)

Wicklow

⌐⌐ = CIVIL PARISHES ADJOINING ACROSS
BARONY BOUNDARIES.

Dublin County Civil Parishes 1 - 83

1.	Balscadden	43.	Grangegorman
2.	Balrothery	44.	St. George's
3.	Skerries or Holmpatrick	45.	Killester
4.	Lusk	46.	Clontarf
5.	Baldongan	47.	Leixlip
6.	Naul	48.	Lucan
7.	Garristown	49.	Aderrig
8.	Grallagh	50.	Esker
9.	Hollywood	51.	Kilmactalway
10.	Ballymadun	52.	Kilmahuddrick
11.	Palmerston(Balrothery W.)	53.	Kilbride
12.	Clonmethan	54.	Newcastle
13.	Westpalstown	55.	Rathcoole
14.	Ballyboghil	56.	Saggart
15.	Killossery	57.	Palmerstown (Uppercross)
16.	Swords	58.	Clondalkin
17.	Donabate	59.	Ballyfermot
18.	Portraine	60.	St. James'
19.	Kilsallaghan	61.	Drimnagh
20.	Killeek	62.	Crumlin
21.	Ward	63.	St. Catherine
22.	Mulhuddart	64.	St. Peter's
23.	Cloghran (Castleknock)	65.	Tallaght
24.	Finglas	66.	Cruagh
25.	Clonsilla	67.	St. Mark's
26.	Castleknock	68.	Donnybrook
27.	Chapelizod	69.	Rathfarnham
28.	Malahide	70.	Taney
29.	St. Margaret's	71.	Booterstown
30.	Santry	72.	Whitechurch
31.	Cloghran (Coolock)	73.	Kilmacud
32.	Kilsaley	74.	Stillorgan
33.	Portmarnock	75.	Monkstown
34.	Balgriffin	76.	Tully
35.	Coolock	77.	Kill
36.	Baldoyle	78.	Dalkey
37.	Glasnevin	79.	Kilgobbin
38.	Clonturk	80.	Killiney
39.	Artane	81.	Kiltiernan
40.	Raheny	82.	Rathmichael
41.	Kilbarrack	83.	Old-Connaught
42.	Howth		

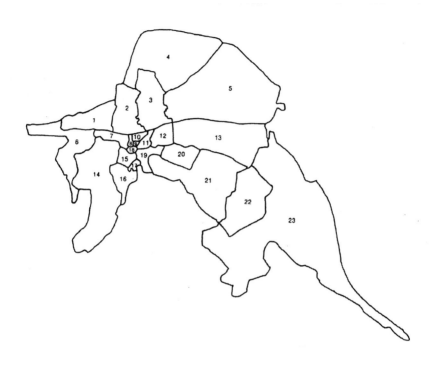

Dublin City adjoining Parishes

01. St. Paul
02. St. Michan
03. St. Mary
04. St. George
05. St. Thomas
06. St. James'
07. St. Audoen
08. St. Michael
09. Christ Church
10. St. John
11. St. Werburgh
12. St. Andrew's
13. St. Mark
14. St. Catherine
15. St. Nicholas' Without
16. St. Luke
17. St. Patrick
18. St. Nicholas' Within
19. St. Bridget
20. St. Anne
21. St. Peter
22. St. Bartholomew*
23. Donnybrook

Note: St. Bartholomew's parish was constituted in 1864 from parts of Donnybrook (St. Mary's) and St.Peter's. Therefore it will not be found in Griffiths Primary Valuations for Dublin as they were carried out between 1848 and 1852.

Superintendent Registrar's District _Dublin South_   Registrar's District _Rathmines_

BIRTHS Registered in the District of _Dublin South_ _Rathmines_ in the Union of _Dublin South_ in the County of _Dublin_

No. (1.)	Date and Place of Birth (2.)	Name (if any). (3.)	Sex. (4.)	Name and Surname and Dwelling-place of Father (5.)	Name and Surname and Maiden Surname of Mother (6.)	Rank or Profession of Father (7.)	Signature, Qualification, and Residence of Informant (8.)	When Registered (9.)	Signature of Registrar. (10.)	Baptismal name if added after Registration of Birth. (11.)
238	1882 Second February 41 Brighton Square West	James Augusta	Male	John Stanislaus Joyce 41 Brighton Square West	Mary Joyce formerly Murray	Government Clerk	Mary Joyce Mother 41 Brighton Square West	Twentieth March 1882	[signature] Registrar	

The birth registration of James Joyce from the birth register held by the General Register Office.
Birth, marriage and death registrations are also available to download from www.irishgenealogy.ie

Chapter 3   Civil Registration

One of the largest and most valuable on-line sources available to the family history researcher is the civil registers of birth, marriage and death held by the General Register Office (www.groireland.ie) which is now located in Roscommon, but has a local office in Dublin.

Civil registration began in Ireland in 1845 with the recording of non Catholic marriages. It was not until 1864 that registration of all marriages, and of births and deaths, commenced. The registers held by the General Register Office are as follows:

Birth Records: All births in Ireland from Jan. 1st 1864, specifying: Child's name; date and place of birth, name of father, occupation of father, name and maiden name of mother and name of the informant.

Marriage Records: Non-Catholic marriages from 1st Jan. 1845, and all marriages from 1st Jan. 1864 specifying: Place and date of marriage, name, age, address and occupation of the bride and groom, name and occupation of father of bride and groom, and witnesses to the marriage.

Death Records: All deaths in Ireland from 1st Jan. 1864 specifying: Date and place of death, name of deceased, marital status, age, occupation, cause of death and details of informant.

GRO On-line
A major proportion of these records is now available free on-line on the government website www.irishgenealogy.ie The records available are:
Births: All records over 100 years: i.e. Currently from 1864 to 1915 and additional years will be added.
Marriages: All records over 75 years old, but currently they are only digitised to 1882. Records back to 1864 will be made available as they are digitised.
Deaths: All records over 50 years old, but currently they are only digitised to 1891. Records back to 1864 will be made available as they are digitised.

The site can be searched by name and/or surname and you can also specify a registration district and a date range. What you will get from this process is firstly a listing of all of the records which meet your description, and also an image of the page of records, which also includes other records from the same date.

For records outside the date available on-line (and for formal certificates of events within these dates), you can order a certificate by mail or email through www.groireland.ie. They are available entirely on-line on this site for events after 1921, but otherwise you must specify the event. If you are unsure of the date, the GRO will conduct a search for a period of +/- 5 years of the date you suggest. However, there are advantages to doing this search yourself and then supplying the GRO with a reference to the certificate you want. This is particularly so if you are searching for a very common name. You can search the index online on www. familysearch.org (see Ireland, Civil Registration Indexes, 1845-1958), or www.Findmypast.ie. The search-form for each allows you to specify dates and names etc. The result will include only the information on the index, but it is enough to get the Volume, Page number and year of the event you are seeking. You can then order from the GRO using these reference numbers. If you do not have much information on parents or dates, and the name is common, you may have to order several certificates to ensure that the correct one is among them.

Registration occurred in Registration Districts. The Registration Districts for County Dublin are: Balrothery, Celbridge, Dunshaughlin, Dublin South, Dublin North, Naas and Rathdown.

Other useful records of possible relevance are held only at the General Registrars Office headquarters in Roscommon. These are:

Births of Irish subjects which took place at sea from 1864. From 1864 to 1885 a separate register is held; from 1886 the index can be found at the back of the main index volume for the relevant year of registration.

Deaths of Irish subjects which took place at sea from 1864. Index (as above)

Births, Marriages and Deaths of Irish subjects serving in the British Army abroad from 1880. Separate index from 1888.

Births of Irish subjects abroad from 1864. No index is available but the registers may be inspected at the GRO. Such births had to be notified to the relevant British Consul abroad.

Access to GRO Records: Some or all of the GRO records may be consulted at the following archives:

General Register Office Research Room, Werburgh Street, Dublin 2. (beside St. Werburgh's Church). Holdings: All registers and indexes as outlined above. G.R.O. birth registrations up to 1916, marriage registrations up to 1941 and death registrations up to 1966 are also available in digital format for download at https://www.irishgenealogy.ie/en/

The National Library of Ireland, Kildare St., Dublin 2, holds the following GRO material:

Deceased Seamen. 1887-1949. Names of seamen whose deaths were reported to GRO specifying: name of deceased; age; rank or profession; official number; name and type of ship; port of registry; cause; place and date of death. From 1893 it includes sex; nationality or place of birth; and last place of abode. (NLI Call no. 31242 d.).

Marriage results for Doyle of Dublin North

Displaying results 901 - 1000 of 1191.

Sorted by Relevance / by Date **Records per page** 10 / 50 / **100**

Marriage of **THOMAS DOYLE** and **MARY FLORENCE** on **30 March 1913**	**Group Registration ID** 1713593 **SR District/Reg Area** Dublin North
Marriage of **PATRICK DOYLE** and **HILDA CATHCART** on **18 February 1913**	**Group Registration ID** 1711553 **SR District/Reg Area** Dublin North
Marriage of **PATRICK DOYLE** and **CATHERINE MCKEON** on **04 February 1913**	**Group Registration ID** 1739245 **SR District/Reg Area** Dublin North
Marriage of **JOHN DOYLE** and **HELENA BYRNE** on **22 January 1913**	**Group Registration ID** 1711222 **SR District/Reg Area** Dublin North

A typical search result from www.irishgenealogy.ie - see page 23

CENSUS OF IRELAND, 1901.

FORM A.

(Two Examples of the mode of filling up this Table are given on the other side.)

RETURN of the MEMBERS of this FAMILY and their VISITORS, BOARDERS, SERVANTS, &c., who slept or abode in this House on the night of SUNDAY, the 31st of MARCH, 1901.

No.	NAME and SURNAME (Christian Name)	(Surname)	RELATION to Head of Family	RELIGIOUS PROFESSION	EDUCATION	AGE (Years)	AGE (Months)	SEX	RANK, PROFESSION, OR OCCUPATION	MARRIAGE	WHERE BORN	IRISH LANGUAGE	If Deaf and Dumb; Dumb only; Blind; Imbecile or Idiot; or Lunatic.
1	Edward	Hegan	Head of Family	Church of Ireland	Read & write	60		M	Farmer	married	Co. Dublin	Irish	
2	Thomas	Hegan	Brother	Church of Ireland	Read & write	54		M	Superannuated R.I.C.	not married	Co. Dublin		
3	Caroline	Hegan	Sister	Church of Ireland	Read & write	58		F	—	not married	Co. Dublin		
4	Elizabeth	Hegan	Sister	Church of Ireland	Read & write	22		F	—	not married	Co. Wicklow		
5	John T.	McCrea	Boarder	Church of Ireland	Read & write	60		M	Land owner	Widower	Co. Dublin		
6	Sarah	Bryan	Servant	Church of Ireland	Read & write	43		F	General Domestic Servant	not married	Dublin		
7	Ellen	Glennon	Servant	Roman Catholic	Read & write	21		F	General Domestic Servant	not married	West Meath		
8	Samuel	Fox	Servant	Church of Ireland	Read & write	40		M	Farm Labourer	not married	Co. Wicklow		
9	Andrew	Butler	Servant	Roman Catholic	Read & write	45		M	Farm Labourer	not married	Co. Dublin		
10	Henry	Leavington	Servant	Church of Ireland	Read & write	28		M	Van driver	not married	Dublin		
11	Martin	Donovan	Servant	Roman Catholic	Read & write	26		M	Farm Labourer	not married	Queens County		
12	Michael	Connor	Servant	Roman Catholic	Read & write	22		M	Farm Labourer	not married	Co. Kildare		
13	John	Cane	Servant	Roman Catholic	Read & write	18		M	Farm Labourer	not married	Co. Dublin		
14	Owen	Daly	Servant	Roman Catholic	Read	53		M	Cattle Drover	not married	Dublin		
15													

I hereby certify, as required by the Act 63 Vic., cap. 6, s. 6 (1), that the foregoing Return is correct, according to the best of my knowledge and belief.

Edward Hegan _____
(Signature of Enumerator.)

I believe the foregoing to be a true Return.

Edward Hegan
(Signature of Head of Family).

Chapter 4   Census and Census Substitutes

This chapter lists official or Government censuses and various types of census substitutes, i.e. sources which list Dublin persons at a particular period. These were carried out for a wide variety of purposes but are very valuable for family research. Some of these sources (or abstracts from them) are available on-line.

Official government censuses of Ireland have been carried out at 10 year intervals since 1821. However, the individual household returns for the years 1821-1851 were destroyed in a fire in the Public Record Office in 1921. Returns for the years 1861-1871 were destroyed by Government in order to protect confidentiality, and the 1881 and 1891 returns were pulped during the First World War due to a shortage of paper. A full set of returns for the 1901 and 1911 censuses are available for public inspection in the NAI. These returns are also available on-line from www.census.nationalarchives.ie (see pages 40, 42 and 43).

The following is a chronological list of Censuses and Census Substitutes, with a description, and where each can be accessed. Note that lists of voters before 1830 are essentially restricted to men owning property. From that year householders, leaseholders and occupants of houses who paid rates were entitled to vote.

1468-85. Dublin Freemen
Freemen of the City of Dublin. SLC film 100228; GO Ms. 490/493, NLI Ms 76-79.

1468-1512 Franchise Roll
Dublin City Franchise Roll. The roll gives the names and occupations of 1,425 people, both men and women, who were granted the right to vote in municipal elections for Dublin City Council.

1575-1774. Dublin Freemen
Freemen of the City of Dublin. NLI Ms 76-79.

1610-24. City Inhabitants
Some inhabitants of City of Dublin. Dun Laoghaire Gen. Soc. J. Vol. 1 (1) 1992. 278-31 & Vol. 1 (2) pp 39-43.

1621. St John's Householders
List of Householders in St. John's Parish who were Rated for Parish cess. Appendix 2 in The Registers of St. John's, 1619-1699. Parish Register Society 1 (1906); SLC film 82407; NLI Ir 9293 p 1

1637. Subsidy Roll Payers
Persons paying Subsidy Rolls in St Catherine's (126 names and amount paid); St James (20); St Stephen (24) and St Andrews (49). NAI M2469.

1646. Householders of St John's
List of Householders for St. John's Parish. Parish Register Society, 1 (1906); SLC film 824047.

1652. County Inhabitants
Inhabitants of the Baronies of Newcastle and Uppercross, districts of Ballyfermot, Balliowen, Ballidowde, Belgard, Bellemount, Blundestown, Butterfield, Carranstown, Crumlin, Dalkey, Deane Rath, Esker, Feddenstown, Finstown, Gallanstown, Great Katherins, Irishtown, Killnemanagh, Killiney, Kilmainham, Kilmactalway, Kilshock, Loughstown, Lucan, Milltown, Nangor, Nealstown, Newcastle, Newgrange, Newland, Palmerstown, Rathgar, Rathfarnham, Rowlagh (Ranelagh), Rockstown, Shankill, Symon, Tallaght, Templeogue and Terenure (gives names, ages, occupations, and relationships). NAI M2476. Published in Ir. Gen. 7(4) pp. 496-504; 8(1) pp 3-14; 8 (2) pp 162-174; 8(3) 322-332; & 8(4) 498-529 - see page 29.

1654-56. County Landholders
Civil Survey. Robert C. Simington, Irish Manuscripts Commission, Vol. 7. SLC film 973123.

1656 Dublin Carpenters
Names 116 officials and members of Guild of Carpenters. Ir. Gen. 8(3) 1992, pp 333-336.

1659. Census
"Census" of Ireland. Edited by S. Pender. Dublin: Stationery Office, 1939. SLC film 924648.

THE INHABITANTS OF RATHFARNHAM

BURGOYNE Darby, gent, aged 35 years, tall stature, brown hair,
Burgoyne Amy, his wife, aged 25 years, ruddy complexion, brown hair,
Fullam Margaret, aged 21 years, short stature, black hair,
Roch Rose, aged 17 years, short stature, yellow hair.

BISHOP James, gent, aged 32 years, tall stature, bright brown hair,
Bishop Margaret, his wife, aged 23 years, tall stature, black hair,
Toole Margaret, aged 18 years, short stature, black hair.

PROUD William, aged 50 years, short stature, brown hair,
Proud Alson, aged 43 years, tallish stature, black hair.

GIBSON David, aged 33 years, short stature, black hair,
Gibson Ellinor, aged 40 years, tallish statue, black hair,
Carey Lawrence, aged 26 years, slender stature, black hair,
Doile Sarah, aged 15 years, dark and brown.

HAWKINS Robert, aged 40 years, somewhat burly and black,
Hawkins Elizabeth, aged 30 years, tallish and brown,
Hawkins Mary, aged 60 years, burly and big,
Smith Mary, aged 14 years, red hair,
Moore Daniell, aged 26 years, middle stature, ruddy and yellow,
Bulgre Nicholas, aged 25 years, flat nosed, tall and brown.

An extract from
'1652 Inhabitants of the Baronies of Newcastle and Uppercross'
see page 28

1660-87. Assembly Rolls
Assembly Rolls of the City of Dublin from 1660 to 1687 and from 1788 to 1803. Gilbert Library. Ms 46-53

1663-67. Hearth Money Rolls
Hearth Money Roll. Kildare Arch. Soc. J. 10 (5): 245-54; 11 (1): 386-466 (also covers parts of Kildare). Extracts for Parish of Taney are in J. Ballinteer FHS Vol. 1 (1) pp 29-30. Extracts for Dalkey, Tullagh, Kill, Killiney and Monkstown in Dun Laoghaire Gen. Soc. J. Vol. 3(1) 1994 pp. 35-39; Hearth Tax Roll for Dublin City 1663 in Analecta Hibernica No. 38, page 49-134. Extracts for Dublin city parishes (with 6+ hearths) in DKPRI Vol. 57 (1936)

1664 Dispossessed Land-owners
Heads of families dispossessed in Cromwellian settlements. (40 Dublin names and locations) Ir. Gen. 4(4) 1971 pp. 275-302.

1665. City Tenants
Rental of lands and other city dues for approx. 60 Dublin streets. 57th. Rept. of DKPRI (1936) Appendix 4, pp 526-558.

1666/7. Hearth Money Rolls in St Catherine's
Payers of Hearth Money in New Row, St John's Lane and Thomas St. in Parish Register. Soc., Vol. V (1908) pp 233-235.

1667-1810. Taxpayers in St Bride's
Valuations and Assessments for various years in St Bride's parish. TCD Ms 2036.

1672-1830. Dublin Quakers
Name, date of admission and occupation of Dublin City Quakers. Ir. Gen. 7 (4) 1989. pp 543-50

1680. Pipe Water Accounts
Dublin City Pipe Water Accounts. Ir. Gen. 7(2) 1987, pp. 201-204.

1684. Inhabitants
Principal Inhabitants of Dublin. Ir. Gen. 8(1) pp. 49-57.

1687. Householders of St John's
List of Householders in St. John's Parish. Parish Register Society 1 (1906): 277; SLC film 824047.

1689-99. Dublin Jacobites
Dubliners outlawed for treason. (names and address) Anal. Hib. Vol. 22. (1960)

1700. Tenants on Forfeited lands.
Tenants on forfeited city and county lands offered for sale. GO Ms 543 (2)

1704/5 Pipe Water Accounts
Dublin City Pipe Water Accounts. Ir. Gen. 9(1) 1994 pp 76-88. (Lists relevant householders alphabetically with trade and address).

1730/31. Dublin Debtors
Names, addresses and occupations of debtors in four Dublin prisons. Dub. Hist. Record VI (1943/4), pp. 76-80 & 157-160; VII (1944/45), pp. 34-38.

1738. A Directory for Dublin.
A listing of approx 3,000 individuals compiled from several sources. Published by Dublin Public Libraries. ISBN 0946841594.

1749-91 Eustace St. School subscribers
List of subscribers, giving names and subscriptions. NLI Ms 409.

1756 A List of Inhabitants of St. Michael's Parish.
Irish Builder Vol. 33 pp. 170-171.

1761 Freemen, Freeholders and Militia
Alphabetical list of freemen and freeholders voting at Dublin election. Dublin; Peter Wilson, 1761. NLI I6551 DUBL. & NLI P 349. Militia List of Co. Dublin etc. NLI GO Ms 680.

1762/3 City Tenants
Rental of the Estate of City of Dublin (178 names, location and rent). in *'History and Antiquities of the City of Dublin'* by Walter Harris Appendix, XVI p 482-495.

1766 Religious Census
Religious Census of Parishes of Crumlin GO 537 (79 names only) & RCB Ms.23; Castleknock RCB Ms. 37 and Taney. NAI M2478; SLC film 258517. Religious census of householders (and number in family) in parishes of Monkstown, Kill, Dalkey, Killiney and Tully. Dun Laoghaire Gen. Soc. J. Vol. 1(4) 1992. p 157-164.

1767 Freeholders/Voters
List of Freeholders in Co. Dublin. NAI M 4912. Voters List for Dublin City. (Dublin: Jas. Hunter 1767); NLI I6551 Dubl.; NAI M 4878

1768. Parliamentary Voters
Records of the Poll, giving names of voters and how they voted in parliamentary Elections of 1768. NLI Ms 9362 - 800 Voters): and NLI MS 9361. (for elections of 1768, 1776, 1783, 1790, 1820, 1823, 1826, 1830, 1832): and NLI P 350.

1771. Wives' Certificates
Wives' certificates of the Benevolent Annuity Co. Lists wife's name, maiden name, parents and residence, father's occupation, also name, address and occupation of husband. NLI GO Ms 543 (i)

1772. Inhabitants of Henry and Marlborough Street.
Inhabitants of Henry Street and Marlborough Street (west side) paying Minister's money, a form of tithe payable to the Church of Ireland. (72 names and Addresses) NAI M4959.

1774-1824. Dublin Freemen
Alphabetical List of the Freemen of the City of Dublin. Ir. Anc. 15 (1) and (2) (1983): 2-133; also NLI ILB. 94133 D2.

1775. Loyal Catholics
Catholic Qualification Rolls Extracts (98 names, addresses, and occupations). 59th. Reprint DKPRI, 50-84.

1776. Rent Roll
Rent Roll for Pavement Tax in Merrion Square. DCLA Ms.117. (A list of the inhabitants of Merrion Street and surrounding streets).

1776. Records of the Poll - See 1768

1776-92. Dublin Tradesmen
Records of Admission of Freemen to Corporation of Saddlers, Upholders, Coach and Harness Makers etc. Dublin, NLI Ms. 82.

1777-1830. Dublin Smiths
Brethren admitted to the Guild of Smiths, Dublin, by Marriage Right, 1777-1830. Reports from Committees. Parl. Papers 1837, Vol. 2 (2): (480): 182.

1778-82. Merchants and Traders
The Catholic Merchants, Manufacturers and Traders of Dublin, 1778-1782. Reportorium Novum 2 (2) (1960): 298-323 (compiled from Catholic qualification rolls; gives name, trade, and address).

1779-1825. Bolger Papers
Papers of Brian Bolger, quantity surveyor. Alphabetical listing of some 1800 clients, with address and type of work done. NAI Open Access.

1783. See 1768 - Records of the Poll

1784. Post Office Staff
Employees of the Irish Post Office. Dun Laoghaire Gen. Soc. J. Vol. 5 (1), 1996 (250 names)

1787-1808 Naval Officers
List of Irishmen obtaining Admiralty passing certs. (75 Dubliners) Ir. Gen. 3 (11) 1966 & 3(12) 1967.

1788-1803. Assembly Rolls
Assembly Rolls of the City of Dublin from 1660 to 1687 and from 1788 to 1803. DCLA Ms 46-53

1790. Records of the Poll - See 1768

1791-1824. Apothecaries Qualified and Prosecuted
Return of 5,043 Persons examined and certified as Qualified by Apothecaries' Hall in Dublin, and of those Prosecuted, 1791-1829. House of Commons Papers (1829) 235, XXII.491. Available on www.dippam.ac.uk.

1792-1837. Dublin Tradesmen
Names of All Persons Admitted to Dublin Trade Guilds (apothecaries, bakers, barbers, surgeons, carpenters, smiths, merchants, tailors, etc.), 1792-1837. Parl. Papers 1837, 11 (161-91): Appendix 3 (gives names, and some fathers and fathers-in-law names)

1793-1794. Loyal Catholics
Catholic Qualification Rolls: Names, addresses and rank/occupation of Catholics taking oath of allegiance. NAI Ref. 2-446-53.

1793-1810. Coolock Protestants
Census of Protestants in Castleknock. SLC film 100225 & NLI GO Ms 495.

1797. Freeholders
Alphabetical list of Freeholders for Co Dublin Parliamentary Election (with abode, freehold, date of registration and comments) NLI Ms 2711.

1798. Rebellion Compensations/ Orangemen/ Householders
List of Persons who Suffered Losses in '98 Rebellion. NLI JLB 94107 (approximately 100 names, addresses, and occupations). Members of Orange Lodge, Dublin (gives name, address (usually) and date of admission. NLI Ms. 5398. Householders of York Street and the Poddle (79 names and addresses). J. Dun Laoghaire Gen. Soc. 5(2) 1996 p. 41-44.

1801. Clonsilla and Mulhuddart Protestants
Protestants in parishes of Clonsilla and Mulhuddart (with children's ages) NLI GO 495.

1805-1839. Pupils of St Kevin's
Register of Pupils of Kevin St. School (inc. name, age, religion, origin, where sent, trade etc.) NLI Pos. 2884.

1806. Parliamentary Voters/ Petitioners
Records of the Poll (names of voters) for Parliamentary Elections. NLI Ms . 6128. Also records of 3,003 voters arranged by Guild membership NLI Ir 94133 d 13 Names of Petitioners: 38 occupants of Castle Street and 19 occupants of Lr. Mount Street. - J Dun Laoghaire Gen. Soc. Vol. 4(2) 1995. p. 82-84.

1807. Tradesmen and Voters
Tradesmen employed by the Board of Works, Dublin. Dun Laoghaire Gen. Soc. J. Vol. 4 (2) 1995 (names and trade description).
Records of the Poll (names of voters) for Parliamentary Elections. NLI Ms . 6129

1809. Freeholders
List of Freeeholders in Co Dublin (name, residence, landlord and residence, value and date of registration) NLI Ms 9361.3

1810. Freeholders
Freeholders in Co Dublin (name, residence, landlord and residence, value and date of registration) NLI Ms 9361.4

1814. Police (RIC)
Royal Irish Constabulary (RIC) members (note also DMP p. 46). The records of all 90,000 members of the RIC are in the Public Record Office in London (Ref. HO 184.43). A copy (Ref. MFA 24/1-16) is in NAI. The records are indexed by initial letter of the surname in two periods i.e. 1816-67 and 1867-1922. The information includes age and date of entry; height; religion, native county; trade; marital status; county of wife; postings; promotions and punishments and dates of same.

1816. City Tenants
Rental (tenant list) of the estate of the city of Dublin. Appendix VIII to "History of the City of Dublin" by Warburton, Whitelaw & Walsh, London 1818.

1817 - 1947 Simpson's Hospital, Applicants for Admission
A record of 'blind candidates for admission', giving name, address, age, and occupation. Published as *'Simpson's Hospital ~ An Establishment for Dispensing Hospitality'* (Ballinteer FHS 2000) - See below.

No.	Name	Age	Occupation	Address	Applic./Date
3967	Bennett, Patrick				May 1923
4044	Benson, Arthur	57	Gardener	38 Carrig Ave.,K'town.	Nov.1928
3917	Bent, Rowland	* 67	Electrician	24 Upr.Buckingham St.	May 1914
1286	Bentley, George	72	Bookbinder	Castleknock	May 1852
2721	Bermingham, John	74	Fruiter's Clerk	30 Marlborough St.	18th Nov.1880
2736	Bermingham, John		Fruitmarket Clerk	30 Marlborough St.	May 1881
2769	Bermingham, John	75	Fruit Clerk	27 Denzille St.	Nov.1882
4410	Bermingham, Patrick	76	Coachman	Iveagh House,Bride's St.	Nov.1945
668	Bernard, Thomas	71	Cabinetmaker	Abbey St.	Nov.1838
3563	Berthistle, Thomas	57	Coal Dealer	25A Nth.Gt.George's St.	Nov.1903
3593	Berthistle, Thomas	58	Coal Dealer	25A Nth.Gt.George's St.	Nov.1904
3617	Berthistle, Thomas	58	Coal Dealer	25A Nth.Gt.George's St.	May 1905

1818. Parliamentary Voters
Records of the Poll (names of voters) for Parliamentary Elections . NLI Ms. 6130

1820. Parliamentary Voters
Records of the Poll (names of voters) for Parliamentary Elections. NLI Ms . 6128. and NLI Ms 9361.

1821. Tallaght Census
Government Census Extracts for Dublin City and Tallaght for Selected Surnames. SLC film 100158; NAI .

1822 – 1852. Darley Estate
133 tenants of estate of Henry Darley in Dublin. Full index. NLI: Ms. 5806

1823 and 1829. Harbour Workers
Kingstown (or Dun Laoghaire) Harbour workers in 1823 (129 names and trades) and 1829 (192 names and trades) Dun Laoghaire Gen. Soc. J. Vol. 6(4) 1997 pp. 114-121; and NAI OPW 8/355 and OPW 8/752.

1821-46. Tithe Applotment Survey (see p.121).

1826. Weavers, Labourers and Fresh Water Petitioners
Weavers and Related Trades in Dublin. Dun Laoghaire Gen. Soc. (1995) ISBN 1-898471-15-0. Extracted from: NAI - SPO OP/588t/727 (1522 names of tradesmen and labourers, including boys of 10-16 years); and NAI - SPO OP/588s/726. (1,004 names of labourers wives receiving benefit). Names (only) of 50 inhabitants of Kingstown petitioning for fresh water. Dun Laoghaire Gen. Soc. J. Vol. 5(1) 1996. p28-30.

1826. Weavers in Balbriggan
Lists the names of weavers in Balbriggan who signed a memorial regarding buildings in Dublin where they may ply their ware. NAI CSORP 1826/13/727, also published in *Weavers of Prosperous, Balbriggan and Tullamore in Memorials of 1826.* Dun Laoghaire Genealogical Society (1998).

1826. Records of the Poll - See 1768

1830. Freeholders
Dublin City and County Freeholders (contains names and addresses). NLI Ms. 11.847. (Domville Papers). see also 1768 - Records of the Poll.

1831. Householders of St Bride's and Clontarf Tithe-Payers
Householders in St. Bride's Parish (possibly based on 1831 census). NLI P1994, original in St. Werburgh's, Dublin. Clontarf Tithe-Payers. (names and amount paid) NLI Pos. 7093.

1832. Voters and Cholera Victims
Names of Freemen Registered as Voters, City of Dublin. Parl. Papers 1837, Vol. 2 (1): 159-75 (2,678 names only). List of the voters of December, 1832, to elect representatives for the University of Dublin in parliament (Dublin: R M Tims, 1833). Gives names, addresses and qualifications of voters. NLI P.650 and NLI Ir 94133 d14. Cholera cases in the Parish of St Thomas. Lists 550 names, address, occupation, age, number in family, date of seizure and how disposed of. NAI M4962.

1832. Records of the Poll - See 1768

1832-36. Parliamentary Voters/ Publicans
A list of the Registered Voters in Parliamentary Elections for the City of Dublin. Parl. Papers 1837, 11 (2) (480): 1-145 (names, occupations, residence, etc., alphabetically by year). Names and Residences of Persons in Dublin Receiving Liquor Licenses. Parl. Papers 1837, 11 (1) Appendix II: p. 250.

1832, 35 and 37. Parliamentary Voters
Alphabetical list of the Constituency (Voters) of Dublin with residence, qualification and profession. Pettigrew and Oulton, Dublin 1837. (Approx. 11,000 names). List of 431 Voters in Dublin City (giving residence, occupation, politics and character). NLI Ms. 783.

1835. Voters and Pensioners
Proceedings at Election for Dublin City (lists voters, address, occupation and qualification) NLI Ir 94133 d12. and NLI Ir 94133 d 14; Chelsea Pensioners resident in Dublin (Name, Regt. and Address) NAI OP 1835/8.

1835-37. Dublin County Freeholders and Leaseholders
Freeholders and Leaseholders and how they voted in 1835, 1837, and 1852. NLI ms. 9363. A list of the £50, £20, and £10, freeholders and leaseholders registered in the county of Dublin, arranged by barony, up to 1st July, 1837 by D. Macnamara (Dublin: Grace 1837). NLI JP 907

1841. Parliamentary Voters
Mirror of the Dublin election for members to serve in parliament July 1841; arranged in street lists. (Dublin: W.H. Dyott, 1841) pp. 296. Gives names, addresses, occupations. NLI Ir. 94133 d.15.

1841 Census Search applications. see page 41.

1842. Parliamentary Voters
List of voters at the city of Dublin election (Dublin: Shaw Brothers, 1842) pp. 27. Gives names, addresses, occupation and qualification. NLI Ir 32341 d15 and d 29.

1842 - 1864. Deserted Children
Deserted children in Parish of St. Thomas. 130 names, where and when found, age, sex and to whom given. NAI M 4962.

1843. Parliamentary Voters
Voters List. NAI 1843/52

1844. Petitioners
Petitioners from the Barony of Dublin seeking barony status change (89 signatures only). NAI OP 1844/10.

1844/50. Householders of St Peter
List of householders in Parish of St. Peter. RCB Library P45/15/1 & 2.

1846/47. Boat-owners of Rush
Boat owners and Fishermen petitioning for a new pier (300+ names only). NAI OPW 8, item 329.

1848. Dun Laoghaire Petitioners/ Orangemen
Kingstown (Dun Laoghaire) Petitioners in support of William Smith O'Brien. 235 names and some addresses. J. Dun Laoghaire Gen. Soc. 4(4) 1995 p. 131-137. Members of the Orange Institute, Dublin petition for clemency for William Smith O'Brien. (Signatures and addresses) NAI OP 1848/251.

1848-54. Griffith's Primary Valuations - see page 122

1850. Millers of Dublin
Mills and Millers (Saw, flour, woollen, paper etc) in Dublin are extracted from Griffith's Valuations and published in *The Millers and Mills of Ireland of about 1850* by William E.Hogg, Dublin (1997) p.183-192.

1850-1854. Deserted Children in Dublin
A listing of children found in Dublin giving details including, name (some unknown) age, where found and remarks. On-line at http://www.findmypast.ie/ also available to download from www.irishfamilyhistorycentre.com

1851. Census: Heads of Household.
List of heads of families in the 1851 Census of Dublin City, compiled by D.A. Chart. NAI CEN 1851/18/1-2. (Gives the name of approx 60,000 heads of household alphabetically by street). A hardcopy typscript, arranged by surname and by street is available in the Dublin City Library and Archive. It is also On-line at http://www.findmypast.ie/

1851 Census Search applications. see p.42.

1852. Parliamentary Voters
Lists of registered voters of county Dublin (Dublin: Browne & Nolan, 1852), pp. 140. Gives names and addresses of 6,349 voters; also NLI Ms 9363. List of voters, Co. Dublin, July 1852. (Dublin: np, 1852). Gives names and addresses (and religion of some). UCD Pamphlets no. 5328. see also 1835-37.

1853. Catholic Petitioners
Memorial from 140 Catholic Parishioners of Clondalkin seeking a new priest. Cullen Papers 46/1/3, Dublin Diocesan Archives.

1857. Trinity Voters
City of Dublin election, March 1857. List of electors (Dublin: Browne & Nolan, 1857). Gives names and addresses of voters and how they voted. BL 809 N. 33; NLI Ir 32341 d16 & d30; TCD Gall. BB 15 30a. Names of the electors at College election, 1857, pp 63. Hand written - gives names, addresses and qualifications of voters. NLI Ms 199.

1859. Local Voters
May 1859. List of electors for City of Dublin election (Dublin: Shannon and McDermott, 1859), pp. 277. Gives names and addresses of voters. BL 809. f. 42; NLI Ir 32341 d.25.

1859 - 1884. Mendicity Institution Admission books
Lists of persons given charitable assistance, with name, age, residence, where born and other details. (Oct 1859- mar 1860) lists of approx. 10,000 names from Oct 1859 to Nov 1884. NLI: Colclough Ms. 32,601

1861-1871 Booterstown Boys School
Register of pupils providing: pupils name, address, date of birth, year of entry, previous school and father's occupation. J. Dun Laoghaire Genealogical Society 1999. see also 1891

1861. Census Search Applicants ~ see 1908

1863/1864. Cess-Payers
Cess Applotment book of Parish of St Thomas. Names of householders, valuations and applotments by street for Easter 1863 and '64. NAI M 4957 and 4958.

1864-1865. Dublin Voters
Voters of Dublin County. (Dublin City is excluded) 2 Registers of persons entitled to vote at Parliamentary elections. (Name, address, qualification to vote, and description of property for Nov. 1864-Dec. 1865) NLI Ms. 6132-3;

1864. Petitioners against closure of Kill of the Grange Cemetery
'*Petitioners against the closure of Kill O' the Grange Cemetery.*' Over 2,200 names and addresses (the vast majority of addresses are given by area, i.e Kingstown, Blackrock etc). - Dun Laoghaire Genealogical Society 1998. Also a list of 153 names and addresses of persons with burial rights for the above cemetery. Jnl. GSI Vol. 13 (2012) p.91-94.

1864-1885. Vaccinated Children
Vaccinations in the Registrar's Districts of Bray and Rathmichael 1864 - 1885. Register includes Child's name, age, vaccination date, parent or guardian and address. NAI LBG 137 L2

1865. Voters
List of 4,700 registered voters of County of Dublin. (Dublin: Browne & Nolan, 1865), Gives names and addresses. Available on Google Books. TCD. List of electors 1865 (Dublin: J. Atkinson, 1865) (Gives names and addresses of voters) NLI Ir 32341 d. 15. Available on Google Books

1868. Local Voters
List of electors for the year 1868 (Dublin: Browne & Nolan, 1868) pp. 361. (Gives names and addresses of voters). also in NLI Ir 32341 d. 16; TCD Library Gall. NN 4 22. Also *City of Dublin Election,* Nov. 18th, 1868 by Tudor S. Bradburne (J. Atkinson, 1869), pp. 272. SLC fiche 6343075

1872-74. Infants born in or admitted to Irish workhouses
Infants born in workhouses or admitted under 1 year of age. Lists names (only) of 600 children in North Dublin Union, 1000 in South Dublin Union and some in smaller workhouses. http://www.dippam.ac.uk/eppi/documents/16483, also available from http://anguline.co.uk/irel.html

1875-77 Malahide and Portmarnock Church of Ireland Parishioners
Malahide and Portmarnock CoI parishioners by street giving names of all family members, occupation, and (in some cases) dates of birth. NLI Ms 1481 (1875/6) and Ms 1482 (1877).

1875. Burial Rights for Carrickbrennan Cemetery, Monkstown
A list of 264 names and addresses of persons with burial rights for the above cemetery. Jnl. GSI Vol. 15 (2014) p.125-128.

1878. Voters and Freeholders
Freeholders, Voters (with residence) and Lodgers (with profession/trade and landlord's name and address). NLI ILB 324d

1881-89 Malahide and Portmarnock CoI Parishioners
Malahide and Portmarnock CoI parishioners by street giving names of all family members, occupation, and (in some cases) dates of birth. NLI Ms 1483 (1881-84); Ms 1484 (1885-88) & Ms 1485 (1889).

1882. Stephen's Green Club Members
A list of names (only) of members of the Stephen's Green Club. NLI Ir 367 s12

1891-1939 Booterstown Boys School - see 1861.

1894-1970 St. Patrick's School, Dalkey
Register of pupils providing name, address, birth date, year of entry, religion, previous school and father's occupation. - Dun Laoghaire Genealogical Society 1999.

1896. Voters of Rathmines and Rathgar
Arranged by street, giving names and addresses. NAI M. 1203.

1901. Government Census Returns
Official Government Census of all households conducted on 31st of March 1901. Includes: Name; Relationship to Head of family; Religion; Literacy; Age; Sex; Occupation; Marital Status; Birthplace; Ability to speak Irish; and Infirmities. NAI

1904-1948 Harold Boys School, Glasthule
Register of pupils, providing the following details: pupils name, address, date of birth, year of entry, previous school and fathers occupation. -Dun Laoghaire Genealogical Society 1998.

1908-1922. *Census Search Applications*

The Pension Act of 1908 allowed persons of 70 years and over to receive an old-age pension. As civil registration of births only began in 1864, birth certificates were not available as proof of age. One method of proving age was to apply for a search of an early census (usually those of 1841, 1851 or 1861), this would show the applicant's age at that time. The applicant's details were completed on census search application forms (or Green Forms). The indexes to these are available and give the name of the family who were claimed to be resident in the census to

A search form for the 1851 census.

be searched. The Green form provides: Name and address of applicant; Parent's names (sometimes mother's maiden name); Head of family if other than father; Relationship and occupation; Parish; Townland/Street and date of receipt of application. NAI and downloadable in pdf file from: http://censussearchforms.nationalarchives.ie/search/cs/index.jsp

1911 Government Census Returns and published abstracts
Official Government Census conducted on 2nd April 1911. Each household return lists, for each occupant: Name; Relationship to Head of family; Religion; Literacy; Age; Occupation; Marital Status; Number of years married; Numbers of births; Birthplace; Languages spoken (i.e. Irish and/or English) and Infirmities. NAI. Available on-line from www.nationalarchives.ie. - See page 43.

1913-1921. Bureau of Military History
A collection of 1,773 witness statements, contemporary documents, photos and voice recordings providing valuable primary sources for the revolutionary period in Ireland. Online at www.bureauofmilitaryhistory.ie

1913-1923. Irish Army Medal Applications
Applicants for medals for services during Irish War of Independence. Requests for searches can be made in writing to: Veterans Allowances Section, Department of Defence, Renmore, Co. Galway. A search facility is available at: http://mspcsearch.militaryarchives.ie/search. aspx?formtype=advanced

1914-1918. Irishmen who died in the First World War.
Irishmen in Irish and British regiments of the British Army (and some for other services) who died in the Great War. Pub. 1923 by the Irish National War Memorials Commission. The 49,400 entries provide: Name; Regiment number; Rank; Place and Date of death; and (usually) place of birth. A copy was placed in every major Irish library. A fully searchable CD with images of every page is available from Eneclann at www.irishfamilyhistorycentre.com Also available on http://www. findmypast.ie/

1916 – 1923. Military Service Pensions Collection.
Lists of veterans who gave active service during the War of Independence and who deemed themselves eligible for allowances or pensions. Online at www.Militaryarchives.ie

No. on Form B. 22

CENSUS OF IRELAND, 1911.

FORM A.

Two Examples of the mode of filling up this Table are given on the other side.

RETURN of the MEMBERS of this FAMILY and their VISITORS, BOARDERS, SERVANTS, &c., who slept or abode in this house on the night of SUNDAY, the 2nd of APRIL, 1911.

No.	NAME AND SURNAME (Christian Name / Surname)	RELATION to Head of Family	RELIGIOUS PROFESSION	EDUCATION	AGE (Males)	AGE (Females)	RANK, PROFESSION, OR OCCUPATION	PARTICULARS AS TO MARRIAGE (Whether "Married," "Widower," "Widow," or "Single")	Completed years the present Marriage has lasted	Total Children born alive	Children still living	WHERE BORN	IRISH LANGUAGE	If Deaf and Dumb; Dumb only; Blind; Imbecile or Idiot; or Lunatic
1	William Fortune	Head of Family	Roman Catholic	Read & write	60		Police Pensioner	Married				Dublin City		
2	Anne Fortune	Wife	Do	Read & write		50		Married	32	9	7	Do		
3	Laurence Fortune	Son	Do	Read & write	30		Book Keeper	Single				Do		
4	William Fortune	Son	Do	Read & write	28		Traveller	Single				Do		
5	Patrick Fortune	Son	Do	Read & write	22		Minor (Coal)	Single				Do		
6	May Fortune	Daughter	Do	Read & write		19		Single				Do		
7	Philip Fortune	Son	Do	Read & write	16		Solicitor	Single				Do		
8	Annie Fortune	Daughter	Do	Read & write		12	Scholar	Single				Do		
9	James O'Mahony	Boarder	Do	Read & write	34		Carpenter	Single				Galway		
10	Eugene Toomey	Boarder	Do	Read & write	27		Motor Electrician	Single				Kerry		
11	Patrick O'Rea	Boarder	Do	Read & write	19		Electrician (Gen.)	Single				Kerry		
12	Clara O'Rea	Boarder	Do	Read & write		17	do	Single				Wexford		
13														
14														
15														

The 1911 census return for the Fortune family of 22 Heytesbury Street, Dublin City.

1917-18. Soldier Patients

Patients at Blackrock Military Hospital (June 1917-Aug. 1918) (Name, rank, Regt., religion) Dun Laoghaire Gen. Soc. J. Vol. 5(4) 1996. p.136-139.

1918. Anti-Conscription Protesters

Names of persons taking anti-conscription pledges in Parish of St Michael and John. Over 1700 names and (usually) address.
NAI M. 2666-74.

1922. Irish Army Census

A census of the Army of the new Irish State in November 1922. Lists: name, address, next of kin, and age. Military Archives, Cathal Brugha Barracks. Search online at: http://census.militaryarchives.ie/

An extract from the 1922 Irish Army Census
of Beggar's Bush Barracks Dublin

1922. County Dublin Farmers

Members of the Farmers Association in Balbriggan (37 persons), Blanchardstown (34), Clondalkin (21), Coolock (55), Donabate (25), Garristown (26), Kilsallaghan (24), Lucan (16), Lusk (56), Naul (26), Old Town (10) and Rush (14). NLI Ms 19, 028.

1924 to date. Irish Army Pension Applications

Applicants for Irish army pensions giving: Name, details of service units and districts. Applications for information to: Veterans Allowances Section, Department of Defence, Renmore, Co. Galway.

General References.

1593-1860. Alumni Dublinenses.

A *'Register of the Students, Graduates, Professors and Provosts of Trinity College, in the University of Dublin from 1593 - 1860'*. Gives details of dates of admission, fathers name and occupation, subject and date of degrees (where relevant) etc. Published by Thom's Dublin 1935. A CD covering the period up to 1846 is available from www.archivecdbooks.ie - See below.

BARRY, WILLIAM. 1743.	BARTON, RICHARD. 1721-22.
BARRY, WILLIAM NORTON, S.C. (Dr French), July 15, 1773, aged 16 ; s. of Richard, Generosus ; b. Dublin. B.A. Æst. 1777. [Irish Bar 1785.]	BARTON, GEORGE, Pen. (Mr Geoghegan), Oct. 12, 1839, aged 17 ; s. of John, Professor Musicæ ; b. Dublin. B.A. Vern. 1846.
BARRY, WILLIAM NORTON, S.C. (Eton Coll.), June 4, 1832, aged 17 ; s. of Richard, Miles; b. Dublin. See *Eton School Lists.*	BARTON, GEORGE ELLIOTT, Pen. (Mr Burke), Oct. 13, 1843, aged 17 ; s. of James, Pragmaticus ; b. Dublin. B.A. Vern. 1848.
BARRY, ZACHARIAH, Pen. (P.T.), Nov. 4, 1844, aged 16 ; s. of David, Medicus, defunctus ; b. Co. Cork. B.A. Vern. 1849. LL.B. and LL.D. Hiem. 1868.	BARTON, GUSTAVUS, Pen. (Mr Huddart), Oct. 16, 1835, aged 23 ; s. of James, Pragmaticus ; b. Dublin. B.A. Vern. 1840. M.A. Vern. 1843.
BARTER, JOHN T., Pen. (Mr Browne), Oct. 14, 1845, aged 22 ; s. of Thomas, Generosus ; b. Co. Cork. B.A. Vern. 1850	BARTON, HUGH, Pen. (Mr Phillips), Oct. 15, 1821, aged 16 ; s. of William, Generosus ; b. Dublin. B.A. Vern. 1827.
BARTON, AUGUSTINE HUGH, Pen. (Mr Smith), Mar. 1, 1830, aged 15 ; s. of Dunbar, Generosus ; b. Tipperary. [Irish Bar 1845.]	BARTON, HUGH, Pen. (P.T.), Dec. 4, 1821, aged 19 ; s. of James, Generosus; b. Middlesex.
BARTON, BAPTIST, S.C. (Mr Fullerton), Oct. 4, 1833, aged 17 ; s. of Baptist, Maine; b. Denotes	BARTON, JAMES, Pen. (Mr Sheridan, Dublin), Feb. 27, 1720-21, aged 18; s. of John, Clericus ; b. Painstown, Co.

1637-1809. Dublin Goldsmiths

Alphabetical list of Dublin goldsmiths with date of admission, plus name of a parent and occupation. GO MS 665.

1703-1838. Convert Rolls

A index by surname of 5,500 people who converted from Catholicism to the Church of Ireland during the period 1703-1838. Edited by Eileen O'Byrne. Published by the Irish Manuscripts Commission (Dublin, 1981).

1760-1901. Changes of Name.

Compiled by W.P.W Phillimore and Edward Fry, primarily based on the Changes of Name by Royal Licence. Extracted from the London Gazette and Dublin Gazette from 1760 to 1901. Arranged alphabetically by the current name followed by original name and in some cases, date and brief comment. Published by S and N Genealogical Supplies. www.genealogy.demon.co.uk

1786-1921. Dublin Metropolitan Police (DMP)

A Police force for Dublin City and adjoining townships which was set up in 1786 and remained independent of the Royal Irish Constabulary (q.v.) which policed the remainder of the country. It was merged with the Royal Irish Constabulary (q.v.) in 1921 to form the Garda Siochana. Its records are held by the Public Record Office in London and a microfilm copy (Ref MFA 6/3) is available at the National Archives (q.v.). The records show the county of origin, height, previous occupation, age at entry, religion, date of marriage, native county of wife, and the postings and ranks held during their career with the DMP.

The Dublin Metropolitan Police ~ a Short History and Genealogical Guide by Jim Herlihy. (Four Courts Press 2001) Includes select lists of those who were killed on duty, who were awarded the King's Police Medal, who transferred from the London Metropolitan Police and the Royal Irish Constabulary to the DMP - as well as those who joined the Garda Síochána on its amalgamation with the DMP in 1925.

Dublin Metropolitan Police (DMP) Prisoners Books: 1905-1908 and 1911-1918. Lists of persons charged with offences. Available online: http://digital.ucd.ie/

1791-1831. Pupils of Baggott Street Charter School

Indexed register of Pupils of Baggott Street Charter School. (inc. name, age, religion, origin, where sent, observations etc.) NLI Pos. 2884.

1791-1957. Orphan Girls

Register of (Girls) Orphan Home, Prussia Street. (Name, age, where born etc.) NLI Pos. 9008.

1798-1836. Pupils of the Santry School

Indexed register of Pupils of the Santry School (inc. name, age, religion, origin, observations NLI Pos. 2884.

Chapter 5   Church Records

As civil registration of births, marriages and deaths only began in 1864, (and non-Catholic Marriages in 1845) we are dependent on the various churches (denominations) for records of birth, marriage and death prior to these dates.

All denominations have their own parish structures and practices for recording of baptisms, marriages and (sometimes) deaths/burials. The quality and availability of records varies between these different denominations. The factors that determine when record-keeping started, and what records were kept, are fully explored in 'Irish Church Records' (Flyleaf Press, Dublin 2001 - www.flyleaf.ie/irchre.htm).

Dublin had congregations of almost all of the denominations that ever existed in Ireland. The major denominations are Roman Catholic (almost 76% of the Dublin population in 1861) and Church of Ireland (21% of the population). Other denominations included Presbyterian (1.8%); Methodist (0.7%), Jewish; Baptist; Quaker etc. Listed below are the surviving church records arranged by civil parish, indicating the time-frame for record availability, and the repositories in which they are held.

Church of Ireland

The Church of Ireland (CoI) records generally start earlier than Catholic records, the earliest being 1619. Although CoI clergy were required to keep records from 1634, most do not begin until after 1750. All parishes are within the Diocese of Dublin. A full account of the types of records kept by the CoI is given by Raymond Refausse in 'Irish Church Records' (Flyleaf Press, Dublin, 2001).

In 1876 the clergy were required to send their records to the Public Record Office for safe-keeping. A significant number of these records were destroyed in a fire in the PRO in 1922. These are indicated as 'Lost'. However copies and abstracts of the lost registers exist for many parishes, and records of many of the city centre parishes had already been indexed and published prior to their destruction. The major such publications were those of the Parish Register Society. Their work was continued by the Irish Memorials Association (IMA) and the RCB Library continues to publish indexed records of Dublin (and other) churches.

Originals or copies of Church of Ireland registers may be in one of several places. They may be in Local Custody (LC) in the parish of origin. These are usually accessible by arrangement with the local clergyman. They may also be held in the RCBL, where they are accessible for research. The RCBL publish a handlist of all available CoI registers, with links to on-line sources at https://www.ireland.anglican.org/cmsfiles/pdf/AboutUs/library/registers/ParishRegisters/PARISHREGISTERS.pdf Both NAI and NLI have collections of abstracts or extracts of registers, but note that there are extensive gaps in many NAI records and only the start and end date are noted below.

As Church of Ireland records were effectively State records the records of marriage (from 1845) are also in the GRO. (see chapter 3)

Finally, note that some of the Parish registers of Dublin City and County have been indexed by the several Heritage Groups in the county. Those indexed are noted as e.g. 'Indexed by SHS, DHG' etc. as appropriate. The records of Dublin Heritage Group, which is no longer active, are available on the website of www.dublinheritage.ie. The currently active Heritage Groups are: Swords Historical Society Ltd. (formerly Fingal Heritage Group) and Dun Laoghaire Heritage Centre (see pp.151 and 153). The following listing of extant Church of Ireland records is arranged according to the Dublin County Civil Parish maps and Dublin City Civil parish Maps on pages 19 and 21.

The first entry is that of the Parish church (preceded by the corresponding map number), followed by other churches, chapels of ease or chapels connected to institutions which fall within the parish of the main entry. Also included are the records from British Army Barracks in various parts of Dublin.

Church of Ireland Records ~ Dublin City

9 Parish of Christ Church *Wine Tavern Street*
Records: b.1740-1994; m. 1717-2005; d. 1710-1866
Status: RCB Library

23 Parish of Donnybrook or Donebroke *St. Mary's, Anglesea Road*
Records: b. 1712-1957; m. 1712-1956; d. 1712-1916
Status: RCB Library; NLI Ms 4167 (Register of b/m/d of Protestants in Donebroke 1712-1739); IMA Par. Reg. Sect. Vol. 11 (m. 1712-1800); Indexed by DLHS.

Pigeon House Fort *Ringsend*
Records: b. 1872-1901
Status: RCB Library

St Matthew's *Irishtown*
Records: b. 1812-1973; m. 1824-1956; d. 1807-1866
Status: RCB Library; Gilbert Lib. (b. 1827-1846 & 1889-1900; d. 1827-1853) Indexed by DHG (b.1899-1900)

St. John the Evangelist *Sandymount*
Records: b.1850-2003; m.1871-2003
Status: RCB Library

12 Parish of St. Andrew *St. Andrew Street*
Records: b. 1877-1989; m. 1672-1819 & 1845-1985
Status: RCB Library; Parish Register Soc. Vol 11 (1913) (m. 1672-1800); IMA Par. Reg. Sect. Vol. 12. (m.1801-1819)

20 Parish of St. Ann *Dawson Street*
Earliest Records: b. 1719; m. 1799; d. 1722
Status: RCB Library (b. 1873-2008; m. 1845-1978; d. 1780-2006); GO Ms. 577 (b. 1719-1813; m. 1799-1822; d. 1722-1822); SLC film 100226; Parish Register Soc. Vol 11(1913) (m. 1719-1800).

7 Parish of St. Audeon *Cornmarket*
Records: b. 1672-2000; m. 1673-2006; d. 1673-1885
Status: RCB Library; also published in the IMA J. Vol. 12 (b. 1672-1692); Gilbert Lib. (b/m/d. 1672-1916); Parish Register Soc. Vol 11(1913) (m. 1672-1800); IMA J. Vol. XX. (d.1672-1693).

134 *The Registers of Christ Church Cathedral, Dublin*

Page Four
1887

Nov 4   George Russell, born 28 Sept, son of Edward Broadberry, alto in C[hrist] C[hurch] C[athedral] Choir, and Sarah, 12 Killeen Rd, Rathmines, Dublin
J.H. Miles, Res[identiary] Canon, Ch[rist] Ch[urch] Cath[edra]l, Dubl[in].

1889

Mar 19   Constance Monica, born 15 Feb, daughter of Cooper Penrose, Captain R[oyal] E[ngineers], and Sylvia Alice, 49 St Stephens Green
William C. Greene.

Nov 8   Gladys Daisy, born 20 Oct, daughter of John Harril Harris, wine merchant, and Hannah, 39 Mountjoy St, Dublin
William Henry Lang.

Nov 20   Cecil James, born 13 Oct, son of Joseph Henry Miles, Residentiary Canon in Christ Church, & Adelaide L.M., 8 Dawson Street
William C. Greene, Dean.

1891

Jan 9   Georgina Olive, born 13 Dec 1890, daughter of Charles Wrixin Kelly, Professor of Music, and Georgina Annie, 30 Mt Pleasant Square
William C. Greene, Dean.

Jan 10   Philip Vivian, born 28 Nov 1890, son of Joseph Henry Miles, Residentiary Canon in Christ Church, and Adelaide L.M., 8 Dawson St
William C. Greene, Dean.

Septh 23   Millicent Edith, born 1 Septh, daughter of Daniel Lowrey, wine merchant, and Edith Mary, Solent Villa, Terenure, Co. Dublin
W. H. Lang.

A page from the 'Registers of the Christ Church Cathedral, Dublin'

22 Parish of St Bartholomew   *Clyde Road*
Records: b. 1868-1967; m. 1868-1992
Status: RCB Library

Beggar's Bush Barracks   *Haddington Road*
Records: b. 1868-1921
Status: RCB Library

19 Parish of St. Bride (Bridget)   *Bride Street*
Earliest Records: b. 1633; m. 1845
Status: RCB Library (m. 1845-1887); also b.1633-1714 in Ir. Gen.
6 (6) pp.711-723; 7 (1) pp.17-30; 7 (2) pp 205-228; & 7(3) pp.358-
377; Parish Register Soc. Vol. 11 (1913) (m. 1639-1800)

Molyneux Chapel   *Bride Street*
Records: b. 1871-1926
Status: RCB Library

14 Parish of St. Catherine   *Thomas Street*
Records: b. 1699-1966; m. 1679-1966; d. 1679-1898
Status: RCB Library; Gilbert Lib. (b/m/d. 1694-1898); Parish
Register Soc. Vol. 5 (1908) (b/m/d. 1679-1715) and Vol 12 (1915)
(m. 1715-1800). "Registers of the Parish of St Catherine, Dublin,
1636-1715" RCB Library (2003) ed. Herbert Wood. Also "Vestry
Records of the Parishes of St Catherine and St James, Dublin, 1657-
1692" Ed. Raymond Gillespie, RCB Library, 2004. Indexed by DHG
(d. 1863-1898)

Harold's Cross Chapel
Records: b. 1871-2000; m. 1904-1988
Status: RCB Library

4 Parish of St. George   *Hardwick Place*
Records: b. 1794-2000; m. 1794-1956; d. 1824-2001
Status: RCB Library

Free Church
Records: b. 1902-1987
Status: RCB Library

1763.

Jan.	8.	Robt Armstrong to Ann Brooke, Cons^ry Ice.
Feb.	13.	Ezekiel Parks to Mary Kinch, Cons^ry Ice.
March	2.	Major Bury to Miss Stirling.
	29.	Capt. Tanner to Miss Wainright, Consistory Ice.
Ap^l	6.	Thos Sharp to Marg^t Collier, Cons^ry Ice.
May	4.	Mr Smyth to Miss Doherty, Cons^ry Ice.
	5.	Mr Gonne to Mrs Gonne, D^o.
	19.	James Rouse to Eliz. Nesbit.

Marriages from the registers of the parishes of S. Marie, S. Luke, S. Catherine,
and S. Werburgh, 1627-1800. Parish Register Society of Dublin (1915).

6 Parish of St. James   *James's Street*
  Records: b. 1730-1960; m. 1742-1963; d. 1742-1989
  Status: RCB Library; SLC film 962524; Gilbert Lib. (b.1730-1849,
  1854-1902; m. 1730-1849; d. 1730-1884). Indexed by DHG (d.
  1849-1884). See St Catherine's for Vestry Records.

  St. Jude's   *Kilmainham*
  Records: b. 1857-1982; m. 1861-1981
  Status: RCB Library; Gilbert Lib. (b. 1857-1900)

  South Dublin Union   *James's Street*
  Records: b. 1864-1898
  Status: RCB Library; Indexed by DLHS (b 1864-1897)

  Richmond Barracks   *Golden Bridge*
  Records: b. 1857-1922
  Status: RCB Library

10 Parish of St. John   *Fishamble Street*
  Records: b. 1619-1878; m. 1619-1878; d. 1619-1850
  Status: RCB Library; GO Ms. 577 (b. 1702-1878; m. 1799-1878; d.
  1621-1850 - with large gaps in b & m records); SLC film 100226
  Also Published: by Parish Register Soc. Vol. 1 (1906) (b/m/d. 1619-
  1699) IMA Par. Reg. Vol 11 (m. 1700-1798). Republished (in 2000)
  by Representative Church Body Library as "Registers of the Parish
  of St John the Evangelist, Dublin, 1619-1699'. ed. John Mills. Also
  "Vestry Records of the Parish of St John the Evangelist, Dublin 1595-
  1658" Ed. Raymond Gillespie, RCB Library 2001

16 Parish of St. Luke   *The Coombe*
  Records: b. 1713-1974; m. 1716-1973; d. 1716-1974
  Status: RCB Library; Parish Register Soc. Vol. 12 (1915) (m. 1716-
  1800)

13 Parish of St. Mark   *Mark's Street/Pearse Street*
  Records: b. 1730-1971; m. 1730-1971; d. 1733-1923
  Status: RCB Library; List of m. (1730-50) in NLI Ms. 18, 319.

3 Parish of St. Mary   *Mary's Street/Wolfe Tone Street*
Records: b. 1697-1872; m. 1697-1880; d. 1700-1858
Status: RCB Library; Parish Register Soc. Vol. 12 (1915) (m. 1697-1800)

8 Parish of St. Michael   *Michael's Lane/High Street*
Earliest Records: b. 1674; m.1663; d. 1678
Status: RCB Library (b. 1674-1686; m.1663-1756; d. 1678-1750); IMA Par. Reg. Sect. Vol. 12 (m. 1656-1800)

2 Parish of St. Michan   *Church Street*
Earliest Records: b. 1701; m.1796; d. 1727
Status: RCB Library (b.1701-1787; m.1796-1956; d.1727-1745); GO Ms. 577 & SLC Film 100226 (b.1701-24; d 1700-1724); IMA Par. Reg. Sect. Vol. 11 (m. 1700-1800);
Parish Register Soc. Vol. 3 (1907) (b/m/d. 1636-1685) & Vol. 7 (1909) (b/m/d. 1686-1700)

18 Parish of St. Nicholas Within   *Nicholas Street*
Records: b. 1671-1866 m. 1671-1865 d. 1671-1863
Status: RCB Library; Indexed by DHG; IMA Par. Reg. Sect. Vol 11 (m. 1671-1800 & d. 1671-1823) & Vol. 12 (d. 1825-1863); SLC film 990993; Gilbert Lib. (b/m/d. 1671-1866)

15 St. Nicholas Without   *St. Patrick's Cathedral*
Records: b. 1694-1861; m. 1699-1854; d. 1694-1875
Status: RCB Library; Indexed by DHG (b. 1807-1842; m. 1807-1842; d. 1807-1818)

17 Parish of St. Patrick's Cathedral   *Patrick Street*
Earliest Records: b. 1677; m. 1708; d. 1687
Status: RCB Library (b. 1677-1868; m. 1708-1840; d. 1687-1869); GO Ms. 701 (d. 1801-1818); SLC film 257807; Parish Register Soc. Vol. 2 (1907) (b/m/d. 1677-1800). Published as "Register of the Cathedral of St Patrick, Dublin, 1677-1869" Ed. J.H. Bernard & Raymond Refaussé. RCB Library (2007) also on FMP.

1 Parish of St. Paul: *North King Street*
Records: b.1698-1987; m.1699 -1982; d. 1702-1892
Status: RCB Library ; d.1702-1718 published in Register Section
of J. of IMA. Vol. 13(1) pp. 360-390; GO Ms. 577 (d. 1717-1730);
SLC film 100226; Gilbert Lib. (b/m/d. 1698-1887)

Arbour Hill Barracks
Records: b. 1848-1922; d. 1847-1884
Status: RCB Library

St. George's Church, Hardwicke Place.
*'Dublin Delineated in Twenty Six views of Principal Public Buildings' (1831),
also facsimile edition, Dublin City Public Libraries, 2006*

21 Parish of St. Peter   *Aungier Street*
Records: b.1669-1974; m. 1670-1975; d.1670-1883
Status: RCB Library (& index); Gilbert Lib. (b.1669-1894, m.
1669-1845, d. 1669-1840 & 1843-1883); Parish Register Soc. Vol.
9 (1911) (b/m/d. 1669-1761). Indexed by DHG (b.1813-1848;
m.1813-1845; d. 1824-1883 - with gaps)

Baggotrath   *Baggot Street*
Records: b. 1865-1923; m. 1882-1923.
Status: RCB Library

Christ Church   *Leeson Park*
Records: b. 1867-1941; m. 1873-1972
Status: RCB Library

Holy Trinity   *Belgrave Road/Church Avenue, Rathmines*
Records: b. 1850-1951; m 1862-1968
Status: RCB Library

Portobello Barracks   *Rathmines*
Records: b. 1857-1922
Status: RCB Library

St. Kevin's   *Kevin's Street*
Records: b. 1883-1980; m. 1884-1977
Status: RCB Library; Gilbert Lib. (b.1883-1900)

St. Philip   *Milltown*
Records: b. 1844-1939; m. 1867-1956
Status: RCB Library

St. Stephen's   *Mount Street Crescent*
Records: b.1837-2000; m. 1862-1956
Status: RCB Library; Gilbert Lib. (b.1837-1912)

Sandford Church   *Ranelagh*
Records: b.1826-1930; m.1876-1977
Status: RCB Library

5 Parish of St. Thomas   *Cathal Brugha Street*
Earliest Records: b. 1740 m. 1740 d. 1740
Status: RCB Library (b.1750-1970; m. 1750-1980; d.1762-1882);
SLC film 990209; Indexed in '*Register of the Parish of St. Thomas,
Dublin, 1740-1791*'. Raymond Refausse, RCBL, 1994.

Missions to Seamen   *Eden Quay*
Records: b. 1961-1981
Status: RCB Library

North Strand
Records: b. 1878-1939; m. 1879-1922
Status: RCB Library

St Barnaba's   *North Lotts*
Records: b. 1866-1932; m. 1874-1930
Status: RCB Library

Trinity Church   *Gardiner Street Lower*
Records: b. 1871-1918; m. 1874-1915
Status: RCB Library; Parish Register Soc. Vol. 4 (1907) (Register
of Provost Winter b. 1650-1660)

11 Parish of St. Werburgh   *Werburgh Street*
Records: b. 1704-1879, m. 1704-1865, d. 1703-1879
Status: RCB Library; Gilbert Lib. (also churchings from 1789-
1817): Parish Register Soc. Vol. 12 (1915) (m. 1704-1800)

Church of Ireland Records ~ Dublin County

34 Parish of Balgriffin
Records: b.1820-2000; m. 1846-2007; d.1821-1945
Status: RCB Library (see also Balscadden)

2 Parish of Balrothery
Records: b. 1783-1958; m. 1798-1965; d.1782-1810
Status: RCB Library; Indexed by SHS

1 Parish of Balscadden
Records: b. 1839-1887; m. 1840-1949; d. 1821-1842
Status: LC; Indexed by SHS; RCB Library (see also Balgriffin)

71 Parish of Booterstown   *St. Philip and James*
Earliest Records: b.1824-; m. 1824
Status: RCB Library (to 1956); Index (m.7.1825-7.1874) NLI
Ms.5668 ; Indexed by DLHS.

26 Parish of Castleknock   *St. Brigid*
Records: b.1710-1959; m. 1723-1956; d. 1714-1963
Status: RCB Library; GO Ms495; SLC film 992664 (1768-1871)

27 Parish of Chapelizod   *St. Laurence*
Earliest Records: b.1808; m. 1812; d. 1813
Status: RCB Library (bmd from 1812); Indexed by DHG (b. 1808-
1899; m. 1812-1898; d. 1813-1899)

Parish of Cloghran - see Cloughran

58 Parish of Clondalkin   *St. John*
Earliest Records: b.1728; m. 1832; d. 1742
Status: RCB Library (b.1721-; m.1732-; d.1724-); Indexed by DHG
(b. 1728-1899; m. 1832-1891; d. 1742-1900)

12 Parish of Clonmethan
Records: b. 1884-1933; m.1853-1917 (see also: Kilsallaghan).
Status: RCB Library

25 Parish of Clonsilla   *St. Mary*
Records: b. 1830-1901; m. 1831-1956; d. 1831-1902
Status: RCB Library; GO Ms495; SLC film 992664 (1830-1871)

46 Parish of Clontarf   *St. John the Baptist*
Records: b. 1808-2003; m.1812-2002; d. 1812-1875
Status: RCB Library

38 Parish of Clonturk:
St. Aidan's Chapel of Ease, Drumcondra
Records: b. 1910-1961
Status: RCB Library

31 Parish of Cloughran or **Cloghran** (Coolock Barony)
Earliest Records: b. 1782-; m. 1738-; d. 1732-
Status: RCB Library (b. 1782-1852 & 1870-91; m. 1738-1852 & 1858-75; d. 1732-1852 & 1872-1938); Indexed (b.1782-1864) by Anglican Record Project - copies in RCBL & Soc. Gen. (London); SLC film 897365 (b.1732-1864); NAI M 5084 (b. 1782-1870; m. 1738-1839; d. 1732-1870).

35 Parish of Coolock   *St. John the Evangelist*
Records: m.1845-1956
Status: RCB Library

62 Parish of Crumlin   *St Mary's*
Earliest Records: b/d. 1740; m. 1764
Status: Published in IMA. J. Vol. 12 (d. 1740-1830); GO Ms. 495; SLC film 990093 (b/d. to 1864; m. to 1845); NAI M5088 (b.1740-1830; m. 1764-1827; d. 1740-1795 & 1807-1829), NAI M 5089 (m. 1832-1863), NAI M5090 (b. 1823-1863) & NAI M5091 (d. 1831-1862). RCB Library (b.1915-1944; m.1846-1997; d.1914-1982): Indexed by DHG (b. 1823-1867; m. 1846-1898; d. 1831-1862)

78 Parish of Dalkey   *St. Patrick*
Records: b. 1877-1903; m. 1872-1984
Status: RCB Library; Indexed by DLHS (to 1900 approx)

17 Parish of Donabate
Records: b. 1811-1911; m. 1814-1848; d. 1817-1850
Status: Indexed by SHS (to 1900 approx); RCB Library

24 Parish of Finglas   *St. Canice*
Earliest Records: b.1658; m.1666; d. 1664-1683 & 1877-1956
Status: RCB Library (b.1658-84 & 1877-1971; m.1666-67 & 1845-1986; d. 1664-1683 & 1877-1956); also b/m/d records 1685-1684 in Ir. Gen. 9(2) pp. 202-209; GO Ms. 578 (b.1664-1688 & 1695-1735 & 1762-1774; m.1666-1715 & 1717-1818; d. 1668-1727); & SLC film 992663 (Extracts; b.1658-1818; m.1667-1780; d. 1668-1727); IMA J. Vol. 11 (d. 1664-1729).
Published Records: "The Vestry Records of the United Parishes of Finglas, St Margaret's, Artane and the Ward, 1657-1758" Ed. Dr Maighréad Ní Mhurchada, RCB Library 2007

37 Parish of Glasnevin *St. Mobhi*
Records: b. 1757-2000; m. 1793-1970; d. 1793-1996
Status: RCB Library

43 Parish of Grangegorman
Records: b. 1816-1940; m. 1830-1956; d. 1833-1834
Status: RCB Library

Female Penitentiary, North Circular Road
Records: b. 1879-1907
Status: RCB Library

Female Orphan House, Charlemont Street
Records: b. 1870-1953
Status: RCB Library

North Dublin Union
Records: b. 1906-1918
Status: RCB Library

3 Parish of Holmpatrick (Skerries) *St. Patrick*
Records: b. 1779-1829; m. 1800-1955; d. 1786-1829
Status: Indexed by SHS (to 1900 approx); RCB Library

42 Parish of Howth *St. Mary's*
Records: b. 1804-1911; m. 1823-1871; d. 1821-1912
Status: RCB Library

80 Parish of Killiney *Holy Trinity*
Records: b. 1829-2000; d. 1831-1878
Status: RCB Library; Indexed by DLHS (b. 1861-1900; m. 1817-1866)

Ballybrack *St. Mathias*
Records: b. 1867-1955; m. 1873-1955
Status: RCB Library. Indexed by DLHS (b. 1829-1864)

19 Parish of Kilsallaghan, Clonmethan and Naul
Records: b. 1806-2004; m. 1813-1913; d. 1817-2003
Status: Indexed by SHS (to 1900 approx); RCBL

81 Parish of Kilternan or Kiltiernan
Records: b. 1817-2000; m. 1817-1999; d. 1817-2001
Status: RCB Library; Indexed by DLHS (to 1900 approx)

48 Parish of Lucan *St. Andrew*
Records: b. 1877-1972 m. 1845-1956 d. 1877-1993
Status: RCB Library; Indexed by DHG (b. 1877-1899; m.1845-1899; d.1877-1899)

4 Parish of Lusk
Records: b. 1809-1957; m. 1817-1849; d. 1811-1958
Status: Indexed by SHS (to 1900 approx); RCB Library

28 Parish of Malahide *St. Andrew*
Records: b. 1822-1990; m. 1825-2007; d. 1822-2000
Status: RCB Library

Extract from the register of St Michan's Church Dublin in 1722

75 Parish of Monkstown   *St. Mary*
Records: b. 1679-1884; 1676-1899; d. 1669-1893
Status: RCB Library; Parish Register Soc. Vol. 6. (b. 1679-1786;
m. 1669-1708 & 1750-1786) & b/m/d 1783-1800 (from parochial
returns); SLC films 962187 & 883674.

Monkstown   *St John*
Records: b. 1869-1885; m. 1878-1981
Status: RCB Library

Blackrock (Carysfort)
Records: b. 1871-2000; m. 1870-1956
Status: RCB Library

Blackrock   *Christ Church*
Records: b. 1855-1958; m. 1878-1959
Status: RCB Library; Indexed by DLHS

Dun Laoghaire   *Christ Church*
Records: b. 1852-1899; m. 1875-1956
Status: RCB Library; Indexed by DLHS.

Dun Laoghaire   *Mariners*
Records: b. 1843-1970; m. 1875-1972
Status: RCB Library; Indexed by DLHS (to 1900 approx)

Glenageary   **St Paul's**
Indexed by DLHC (b. 1890-1900)

22 Parish of Mulhuddart   *St. Thomas*
Records: m. 1871-1944
Status: RCB Library

6 Parish of Naul
Records: b. 1898-1913; m. 1847-1913 (see also Kilsallaghan).
Status: RCB Library

54 Parish of Newcastle-Lyons
Records: b. 1768-1847; m.1772-1946; d.1776-1847
Status: RCB Library; Indexed by DLHS (to 1900 approx)

33 Parish of Portmarnock
Records: b. 1820-1876; m. 1825-1951; d. 1820-1875
Status: RCB Library

40 Parish of Raheny   *All Saints*
Records: b. 1816-1932; m. 1817-1956; d. 1815-1851
Status: RCB Library

55 Parish of Rathcoole
Earliest Records: b.1891; m. 1846; d. 1890
Status: RCB Library (m.1846-1956); Indexed by DHG (b. 1891-
1899; m.1846-1898; d. 1890-1900)

69 Parish of Rathfarnham
Records: b.1873-1946; m. 1844-1922; d. 1873-1968
Status: RCB Library

Zion Church, Rathgar
Records: b.1885-1950; m. 1885-1898
Status: RCB Library

82 Parish of Rathmichael
Records: b. 1865-1955; m. 1864-1986; d.1893-1915
Status: RCB Library; Marriages (1864-1919) with names and
addresses of bride and groom in Jnl. Dun Laoghaire Gen. Soc. 6(1)
1997, pp 19-22.

30 Parish of Santry
Records: b.1754-1996; m. 1754-1993; d.1753-1952
Status: RCB Library; SLC films 962187, 883674. See Cloghran re
Index.

74 Parish of Stillorgan
Records: b.1876-1948; m.1845-1956
Status: RCB Library

16 Parish of Swords
Records: b. 1705-1843; m. 1793-1842; d. 1725-1826
Status: RCB Library; Indexed by SHS (1750-1899)

65 Parish of Tallaght
Records: b.1889-1970; m. 1845-1956
Status: RCB Library

70 Parish of Taney
Records: b.1791-1967; m. 1795-1998; d. 1814-1950
Status: RCB Library

76 Parish of Tullow or Tully (aka Bullock)
Records: b.1864-1974; m. 1867-1997; d.1891-1953
Status: RCB Library

72 Parish of Whitechurch
Records: b. 1824-1945; m. 1827-1985; d.1824-1933
Status: RCB Library

Huguenot Records

Huguenots were French Protestants who settled in various places across Ireland from 1662 with the assistance of the English Government financial support. The extensive records kept by the Huguenot congregations are described in *'Irish Church Records'* (Flyleaf Press 2001). The following Dublin registers exist:

French Conformed Churches of St Patrick and St Mary
St Patrick Records: b. 1668-87; m. 1680-1716; d. 1680-1716
St Mary Records: b. 1705-16; m. 1705-15; d. 1705-15
United Churches Records: b. 1716-1818; m. 1716-88; d. 1716-1830.
Status: Published by Huguenot Society of London Vol. 7 & 14.

French Non-Conformist Churches of Lucy Lane and Peter Street.
Records: b. 1701-1731 ; m. 1702-1728; d. 1702-1731 & 1771-1831 & Reconnaissance's 1716-1730.
Status: Published by Huguenot Society of London Vol. 7 & 14.
also 'Index to the Account of the French Church in the Lady Chapel of St Patrick's Cathedral 1666-18186. - 200 Names only. GO Ms. 577.

Peter Street Cemetery – Non-Conformist French Huguenot Church...Dublin 1711-1879 by Mona Germaine (Dublin 1999) includes
b. 1701-1731; m.1703-1728 and Bur. 1702-1731 & 1771-1831.

Presbyterian Records

A full account of the types of records kept by the Presbyterian congregations is given by Christine Kineally in *'Irish Church Records'* (Flyleaf Press, Dublin, 2001). Another useful source of background information is 'Congregations in the Presbyterian Church of Ireland (1610-1982)' PHSI (Belfast, 1982).

Presbyterian registers rarely contain death records, and occasionally have only records of baptisms. This is indicated where appropriate. Some of the Presbyterian registers have been indexed by the Heritage Centres in Dublin City and County (see p.151).

Abbey Church
Earliest Records: b. 1777
Status: LC

Arran Quay
Earliest Records: b. 1731; m. 1732
Status: LC; Indexed by SHS (b 1731-1878; m 1732-1900)

Clontarf
Earliest Records: b. 1836
Status: LC; Indexed by SHS

Eustace Street
Earliest Records: b. 1653-1867
Status: LC; SLC film 100238

Lucan
Earliest Records: b. 1875-1900
Status: LC; Indexed by DHG (b.1875-1899

Strand Street
Earliest Records: b. 1767-1867
Status: LC; SLC film 100238

Ormond Quay
Earliest Records: b. 1787
Status: LC

Methodist

An account of the Methodist church in Ireland is given in *'Irish Church Records'* (Flyleaf Press, Dublin, 2001). There are several congregations in Dublin and several registers have been indexed by the Heritage centres serving the county (See p.150). See also: http://methodisthistoryireland. org/family-history-genealogy/

Stephens Green, Centenary Church
Earliest Records: 1864
Status: LC; Register of baptisms (1864-1979) in NLI Pos. 7630

Clontarf
Earliest Records: b. 1876; m. 1870
Status: LC; Indexed by SHS

Skerries
Earliest Records: m. 1889
Status: LC; Indexed by SHS

Baptist Church Records

The Irish Baptist community has always been very small and their records are preserved within each church. The Irish Baptist Historical Society, (see www.irishbaptistcollege.co.uk) can provide information. An account of the records of the Irish Baptist Church is given by Dr. H.D. Gribben in *'Irish Church Records'* (Flyleaf Press, Dublin 2001). Published records 1838 - 1880 include: Register of *Members (1887-1928), Births (1838-72), Marriages (1837-80)* and *Deaths (1841-77)* of Baptist Church, Abbey Street, Dublin. Members of Baptist Chapel, Harcourt Street, Dublin 1887-1928. NLI P.5647

Dublin Unitarian Church

The Dublin Unitarian Church Collection: records of Unitarian congregations at Wood Street, Cook Street, Eustace Street, Strand Street, and St. Stephen's Green. The collection includes minute books, financial accounts, school registers, correspondence, legal papers, sermons etc. Held by the Royal Irish Academy. See www.ria.ie for on-line catalogue and access.

Congregational Church Records

The Irish Congregational Church was very small. The following records of Kingstown Congregational Church have been published in the DLGS journal (now the J. Gen Soc I)
Membership Roll 1849-1861. Dun Laoghaire Gen. Soc. Vol. 2 (1) 1993
Baptisms 1849 -1861. Dun Laoghaire Gen. Soc. Vol. 2 (2) 1993
Baptisms 1881 -1911. Dun Laoghaire Gen. Soc. Vol. 3 (1) 1994
Marriages 1849 -1851. Dun Laoghaire Gen. Soc. Vol. 2 (2) 1993

Roman Catholic

Church records are undoubtedly the most important source of early information for Roman Catholic ancestors. Although the Catholic church was severely restricted during the 18th century in many parts of Ireland, Dublin churches survived, albeit in low profile. A full account of the nature and history of Catholic Church records is in *'Irish Church Records* (Flyleaf Press, Dublin, 2001).

Most RC registers are available free online at http://registers.nli.ie and are also accessible on the commercial websites www.ancestry.com and www.findmypast.ie. Some city centre parishes are available free on www.irishgenealogy.ie Original records are held in their parish of origin, and may be inspected there by appointment.

Indexes and Microfilms:
Indexes of most records have been compiled by one of the Heritage Centres that operate in the county (see P 150); The two centres in Dublin currently offering a service are Swords Historical Society Ltd (SHS) and Dun Laoghaire Heritage Society (DLHS). The records of Dublin Heritage Group (which is no longer active) are available for searching on the website www.dublinheritage.ie.
Microfilm copies of most registers (up to 1880) are also available in the National Library of Ireland (NLI), and through the LDS Library system. Registers of a small number of city churches are not available from either of the above but a search will be made (for a fee) by application directly to the church.

Identifying a Dublin City Parish:
Identifying a Roman Catholic parish in Dublin City can be confusing because both the City civil parishes and the RC church parishes are

called by Saint names. Also, there is not always a correlation between the name of the RC church parishes and the name of the civil parishes. For instance, the Civil Parish of St. Anne's is mainly served by the RC church parish called St. Andrew's etc. To establish which RC parish serves which Civil Parish check the following listing and then consult the RC church records for Dublin City from page 68.

Civil Parish	RC Parish (or parts)
Christchurch	St. Nicholas Without
Donnybrook	Donnybrook
St. Andrew	St. Andrew Ss. Michael and John
St. Anne	St Andrew
St. Audeon	St. Audeon
St. Bartholomew	Donnybrook
St. Bride	Ss. Michael and John St. Nicholas Without
St. Catherine	St. Catherine
St. George	St. Michan St. Mary
St. James	St. James
St. Luke	St. Nicholas Without
St. Mark	St. Andrew
St. Mary	St. Michan St. Mary
Ss. Michael and John	Ss. Michael and John
St. Michan	St. Michan St. Paul
St. Nicholas Within	St. Nicholas Without Ss. Michael and John
St. Nicholas Without	St. Nicholas Without
St. Patrick	St. Nicholas Without
St. Paul	St. Michan St. Paul
St. Peter	St. Andrew Ss. Michael and John St. Nicholas Without
St. Thomas	St. Mary
St. Werburgh	Ss. Michael and John

Roman Catholic Church Records ~ Dublin City

The following records are arranged alphabetically by RC church parish. Some RC parishes cross the boundaries of two or more civil parishes. *See Identifying a Dublin City Parish* on page 66.

RC Parish: Cabra,
Earliest Record: b. 1909; m. 1856
Status: LC
see also: St. Paul's, Arran Quay

RC Parish: St Agatha's   N. William Street
Earliest Record: b. 12.1852; m. 1.1853
Status: LC; NLI (mf); to be indexed by DHG
see also: St. Mary's Pro-Cathedral; St Laurence O'Toole, Seville Place

RC Parish: St. Andrew's   Westland Row
Earliest Record: b. 1.1742; m. 2.1742 (with signficant gaps)
Missing Dates: b. 1752-75, 1789-98, 1803-1848: m. 1752-1798, 1804-
Status: LC; NLI (mf); indexed by DHG (b. 1742-1858; m. 1742-1804)

RC Parish: St. Audoen   High Street
Earliest Record: b. 12.1778; m. 2.1747
Missing Dates: b. 12.1799-6.1800, 9.1856-6.1878; m. 8.1785-1.1800
Status: LC; NLI (mf); partially indexed by DHG

RC Parish: St. Catherine's   Meath Street
Earliest Record: b. 5.1740; m. 5.1740
Missing Dates: b. 2.1794-12.1797, 7.1866-6.1871; m. 12.1792-2.1794, 7.1794-12.1799
Status: LC; NLI (mf); Indexed by DHG (b. 1859-1895; m. 1815-1827)

RC Parish: Donnybrook
Earliest Record: b. 1871; m. 1877
Status: LC; to be indexed by DHG
see also: Sandymount; Haddington Road (St. Mary's)

RC Parish: St Mary's   Haddington Road
Earliest Record: b. 1798; m. 1798
Status: LC; NLI (mf); Indexed by DHG (b. & m. 1798-1876)
see also: Donnybrook; Sandymount

RC Parish: St. James'   James's Street.
Earliest Record: b. 9.1752; m. 1754
Missing Dates: b. 9.1798-1.1803; m. 1755-10.1804
Status: LC; NLI (mf)

RC Parish: St. John
see Ss. Michael and John

RC Parish: St. Kevin's   Harrington Street
Earliest Record: b. 1865; m. 1865
Status: LC; NLI (mf) (inc. Index 1865-1901)

RC Parish: St Laurence O'Toole,   Seville Place
Earliest Record: b. 7.1853; m. 6.1856
Status: LC; NLI (mf)
see also: St. Mary's Pro-Cathedral; St Agatha's, N. William Street

RC Parish: St. Mary's Pro-Cathedral   Marlborough Street
also part St. Michan's
Earliest Record: b. 1734; m. 1734
Status: LC; NLI (mf) (from 1741)
see also: St Laurence O'Toole, Seville Place and St Agatha's, North William
Street

RC Parish: St. Michan's,   Halston Street/North Anne Street
Earliest Record: b. 1726; m. 1726
Status: LC; NLI (mf)

RC Parish: Ss. Michael and John   Lower Exchange Street
Earliest Record: b. 1.1768; m. 1.1784 (marriage index 1743-1842 in register)
Status: LC; NLI (mf) (inc. marriage index 1743-1842); Indexed by DHG

RC Parish: St. Nicholas Without   Francis Street
Earliest Record: b. 1.1742; m. 9.1767; d. 4.1829
Missing Dates: b. 8.1752-1.1767; d. 5.1856-12.1857
Status: LC; NLI (mf); Indexed by DHG
see also St. Kevin's, Harrington Street

RC Parish: St. Paul's,   Arran Quay
Earliest Record: b. 1731; m. 1731
Status: LC; NLI (mf) (inc. Indexes for various set of years)
see also: Cabra

RC Parish: Sandymount,
Earliest Record: b. 1865; m. 1865
Status: LC; to be indexed by DHG
see also: Donnybrook; Haddington Road (St. Mary's)

Identifying a Dublin County Parish:
Identifying a Roman Catholic parish in Dublin County (or County Dublin) is straightforward enough. First consult the *'Townland Index'* (see p.13) to establish the Civil Parish in which your ancestors townland, village or town was located. Then, check for the relevant RC Church Records below.

Roman Catholic Church Records ~ Dublin County

The following records are arranged alphabetically by Civil Parish. Some civil parishes are served by more than one Church Parish this is indicated by a number following the Civil Parish name.

49 Civil Parish of Aderrig
   RC Parish: see Lucan

39 Civil Parish of Artaine
   RC Parish: see Clontarf

 5 Civil Parish: Baldongan
   RC Parish: Skerries, see Holmpatrick

36 Civil Parish of Baldoyle
   RC Parish: Baldoyle (also Howth and Kinsealy)
   Earliest Record: b. 12.1784; m. 1.1785
   Missing Dates: b. 12.1800-8.1806; m. 12.1800-8.1806, 11.1815-5.1818, 11.1824-1.1826
   Status: LC; NLI (mf); Indexed by SHS

34 Civil Parish of Balgriffin
   RC Parish: see Baldoyle

14 Civil Parish of Ballyboghil or Ballyboughal
RC Parish: Indexed by SHS (1832-1899); see Finglas for earlier records

59 Civil Parish of Ballyfermot
RC Parish: part Palmerstown, part Clondalkin

10 Civil Parish of Ballymadun
RC Parish: see Garristown

2 Civil Parish of Balrothery (1)
RC Parish: Balrothery and Balscadden: also Balbriggan (see below)
Earliest Record: b. 10.1816; m. 2.1817
Status: LC; NLI (mf); Indexed by SHS

2 Civil Parish of Balrothery (2)
RC Parish: Balbriggan
Earliest Record: b. 7.1770 (with gaps);   m. 7.1770 (with gaps)
Missing Dates: b, 1778-7.1796; 10.1813-10.1816; m. 6.1810-2.1817
Status: LC; NLI (mf)

1 Civil Parish of Balscaddan
RC Parish: see Balrothery

71 Civil Parish of Booterstown (1)
RC Parish: Booterstown: see also Blackrock at (2) below
Earliest Record: b. 1755; m. 1756
Status: LC; NLI (mf); Indexed by DLHS

71 Civil Parish of Booterstown (2)
RC Parish: Blackrock
Earliest Record: b. 1854; m. 1922
Status: LC; Indexed by DLHS (b. 1854-1900)

26 Civil Parish of Castleknock
RC Parish: Blanchardstown
Earliest Record: b. 1771; m. 1771
Status: LC; NLI (mf) (from 1774); Indexed by SHS

27 Civil Parish of Chapelizod
RC Parish: Chapelizod: see Clondalkin for earlier records
Earliest Record: b. 10.1849; m.11.1849
Status: LC; NLI (mf); Indexed by DHG

23 Civil Parish of Cloghran (near Castleknock)
RC Parish: see Castleknock

31 Civil Parish of Cloghran (near Santry)
RC Parish: see Clontarf (Coolock for later records)

58 Civil Parish of Clondalkin
RC Parish: Clondalkin, Lucan and Palmerstown (separate parishes in later years)
Earliest Record: b. 5.1778; m. 6.1778
Missing Dates: b. 4.1800-6.1812; m. 2.1800-8.1812
Status: LC; NLI (mf); Indexed by DHG

12 Civil Parish of Clonmethan
RC Parish: Rolestown, see Killossery

25 Civil Parish of Clonsilla
RC Parish: see Castleknock

46 Civil Parish of Clontarf
RC Parish: Clontarf
Earliest Record: b. 1774; m. 1774
Status: LC; Indexed by SHS

38 Civil Parish of Clonturk (Drumcondra)
RC Parish: Fairview, see Clontarf for earlier records
Earliest Record: b. 6.1879; m. 6.1879
Status: LC; NLI (mf); Indexed by SHS

35 Civil Parish of Coolock
RC Parish: Coolock, see Clontarf for earlier records
Earliest Record: b. 1879; m. 1879
Status: LC; Indexed by SHS

66 Civil Parish of Cruagh
RC Parish: see Rathfarnham

62 Civil Parish of Crumlin
RC Parish: Rathfarnham and Crumlin - see Rathfarnham

78 Civil Parish of Dalkey
RC Parish: Dalkey: Earlier records in Kingstown, see Monkstown
Earliest Record: b. 1861; m. 1894
Status: LC; NLI (mf); Indexed by DLHS (b. 1861-1900)

17 Civil Parish of Donabate
RC Parish: Donabate:
Earliest Record: b. 11.1760; m. 1.1761
Missing Dates: b. 12.1807-7.1824; m. 6.1805-2.1869
Status: LC; NLI (mf); Indexed by SHS

68 Civil Parish of Donnybrook
RC Parish: part Donnybrook, see Donnybrook Dublin City section;
part Booterstown

61 Civil Parish of Drimnagh
RC Parish: see Clondalkin

Civil Parish of Dublin City
RC Parish: see separate listing - p.68.

50 Civil Parish of Esker
RC Parish: see Lucan, Palmerstown, and Clondalkin

24 Civil Parish of Finglas
RC Parish: Finglas and St. Margaret's:
Earliest Record: b. 2.1784; m. 11.1757
Missing Dates: m. 7.1760-12.1784
Status: LC; NLI (mf); Indexed by SHS

7 Civil Parish of Garristown
RC Parish: Garristown (also Rolestown - see Killossery)
Earliest Record: b. 1.1857; m. 7.1857
Status: LC; NLI (mf); Indexed by SHS

37 Civil Parish of Glasnevin
RC Parish: part Arran Quay (Dublin City) indexed by SHS (b 1731-1878; m 1732-1900); part Finglas

8 Civil Parish of Grallagh
RC Parish: see Garristown

43 Civil Parish of Grangegorman
RC Parish: St. Paul's (Dublin City)

9 Civil Parish of Hollywood
RC Parish: see Garristown or Balrothery

3 Civil Parish of Holmpatrick or Skerries
RC Parish: Holmpatrick (Skerries)
Earliest Record: b. 10.1751; m. 6.1751
Status: LC; NLI (mf); Indexed by SHS

42 Civil Parish of Howth
RC Parish: Howth, see Baldoyle for earlier records
Earliest Record: b. 1890; m. 1890
Status: LC; Indexed by SHS

41 Civil Parish of Kilbarrack
RC Parish: see Baldoyle

53 Civil Parish of Kilbride
RC Parish: Kilbride and Barndarrig (see also Clondalkin for earlier records)
Earliest Record: b. 1858; m. 1858
Status: LC; NLI (mf)

79 Civil Parish of Kilgobbin
RC Parish: Ballybrack (also see Taney; and Glasthule - See Monkstown 3)
Earliest Record: b. 1860; m. 1860
Status: LC; NLI (mf)

77 Civil Parish of Kill
RC Parish: Cabinteely: see also Booterstown
Earliest Record: b. 1859; m. 1859
Status: LC; Indexed by DLHS (b. 1862-1900)

20 Civil Parish of Killeek
RC Parish: see Finglas

45 Civil Parish of Killester
RC Parish: see Clontarf

80 Civil Parish: Killiney
RC Parish: Kingstown (Dun Laoghaire): see Monkstown. Also Ballybrack see Kilgobbin

15 Civil Parish of Killossery
RC Parish: Rolestown (see also Garristown)
Earliest Record: b. 1.1857; m. 1.1857
Status: LC; NLI (mf); Indexed by SHS

51 Civil Parish of Kilmactalway
RC Parish: see Lucan and Clondalkin

73 Civil Parish of Kilmacud
RC Parish: see Booterstown

52 Civil Parish of Kilmahuddrick
RC Parish: see Clondalkin

19 Civil Parish of Kilsallaghan
RC Parish: part Finglas; part Rowlestown, see Killossery

81 Civil Parish of Kiltiernan
RC Parish: Sandyford, see Taney

32 Civil Parish of Kilsaley
RC Parish: see Baldoyle

47 Civil Parish of Leixlip
RC Parish: Leixlip, Co. Kildare
Status: LC; indexed at www.kildare.ie/genealogy

48 Civil Parish of Lucan
RC Parish: Lucan (part of Clondalkin in earlier years)
Earliest Record: b/m fragments for 1835-1837; b. 4.1885; m. 9.1887
Status: LC; NLI (mf); Indexed by DHG to 1901

4 Civil Parish of Lusk (1)
RC Parish: Lusk: also Rush, see below
Earliest Record: b. 9.1757; m. 11.1757
Missing Dates: b. 8.1801-3.1802, 12.1835-8.1856; m. 1.1801-3.1802, 12.1835-3.1856
Status: LC; NLI (mf); Indexed by SHS

4 Civil Parish: Lusk (2)
RC Parish: Rush
Earliest Record: b. 9.1785; m. 9.1785
Missing Dates: b. 12.1796-12.1799; m. 4.1810-8.1813
Status: LC; NLI (mf); Indexed by SHS

28 Civil Parish of Malahide
RC Parish: Malahide (see Swords for earlier records)
Earliest Record: b. 1856; m. 1856
Status: LC; NLI (mf) (Inc. Index 1856-1901); Indexed by SHS (1856-1900)

75 Civil Parish of Monkstown (1)
RC Parish: Monkstown:- earlier records in Kingstown (see below); also Glasthule (see below) also see Booterstown; also Cabinteely, see Kill;
Earliest Record: b. 1855; m. 1865
Status: LC; NLI (mf); Indexed by DLHS (b. 1855-1900; m. 1865-1900)

75 Civil Parish of Monkstown (2)
RC Parish: St Michael's, Dun Laoghaire (Kingstown)
Earliest Record: b. 1755; m. 1755
Status: LC; NLI (mf) (b.12.1768; m. 1.1769); Indexed by DLHS (1755-1900)

75 Civil Parish of Monkstown (3)
RC Parish: Glasthule
Earliest Record: b. 1865; m. 1865
Status: LC; Indexed by DLHS (b.1865-1900)

22 Civil Parish of Mulhuddart
RC Parish: see Castleknock

6 Civil Parish of Naul
RC Parish: Indexed by SHS (1832-1899); see Balrothery for earlier records

54 Civil Parish of Newcastle
RC Parish: see Saggart

83 Civil Parish of Old Connaught
RC Parish: Bray, Co. Wicklow (see also Monkstown)
Earliest Record: b. 1792; m. 1792
Status: LC; Indexed by Wicklow Family History Centre, Wicklow Historic Gaol, Killmantin Hill, Wicklow Town, Ireland. e-mail: wfh@eircom.net; www.wicklow.ie/familyhistorycentre/

11 Civil Parish of Palmerston (Balrothery West)
RC Parish: Rowlestown, see Killossery

57 Civil Parish of Palmerstown (Uppercross)
RC Parish: Palmerstown (see also Clondalkin)
Earliest Record: b. 8.1798; m. 9.1837
Missing Dates: b. 12.1799-9.1837, ends 1862; m. ends 9.1857
Status: LC; NLI (mf); Indexed by DHG (b.1798-1862; m.1837-1858)

33 Civil Parish of Portmarnock
RC Parish: see Baldoyle

18 Civil Parish of Portraine or Portrane
RC Parish: see Donabate

40 Civil Parish of Raheny
RC Parish: see Clontarf

55 Civil Parish of Rathcoole
RC Parish: see Saggart

69 Civil Parish of Rathfarnham (1)
RC Parish: Rathfarnham and Crumlin; see also Terenure and Bohernabreena - see below
Earliest Record: b. 1777; m. 1777
Missing Dates: b/m: 1788-1807
Status: LC; NLI (mf); Indexed by DHG (b.1777-1857; m. 1777-1864)

69 Civil Parish of Rathfarnham (2)
RC Parish: Terenure
Earliest Record: b. 1870; m. 1894
Status: LC; NLI (mf)

69 Civil Parish of Rathfarnham (3)
RC Parish: Bohernabreena
Earliest Record: b. 1868
Status: LC; Indexed by DHG (b. 1868-1901)

82 Civil Parish of Rathmichael
RC Parish: see Taney; also Kingstown, see Monkstown

56 Civil Parish of Saggart
RC Parish: Saggart
Earliest Record: b. 10.1832; m. 5.1832
Status: LC; NLI (mf); Indexed by DHG (to 1899)

67 Civil Parish of St. Mark's
RC Parish: Donnybrook, see Donnybrook, Dublin City section

29 Civil Parish of St. Margaret's
RC Parish: see Finglas

64 Civil Parish of St. Peter's (1)
RC Parish: Rathmines, see St. Nicholas Without, Dublin City section, for earlier records; also Rathgar, see below.
Earliest Record: b. 1823; m. 1823
Status: LC; NLI (mf) (inc index 1823-1881)

64 Civil Parish of St. Peter's (2)
RC Parish: Rathgar, see Rathmines for earlier records
Earliest Record: b.1874; m.1874
Status: LC; NLI (mf)

30 Civil Parish of Santry
RC Parish: see Clontarf; also part Finglas

74 Civil Parish of Stillorgan
RC Parish: see Booterstown

16 Civil Parish of Swords
RC Parish: Swords
Earliest Record: b.12.1763; m. 10.1763
Missing Dates: b.7.1777-6.1802; m. 6.1777-6.1802
Status: LC; NLI (mf); Indexed by SHS

65 Civil Parish of Tallaght
RC Parish: see Rathfarnham; also part Saggart

70 Civil Parish of Taney (1)
RC Parish: Taney or Sandyford, and Glencullen, also part Dundrum
(see below)
Earliest Record: b.1823; m.1823
Status: LC; NLI (mf) (1823-1905); Indexed by DHG (b. 1823-1900;
m 1823-1856; d. no dates)

70 Civil Parish of Taney (2)
RC Parish: Dundrum
Earliest Record: b. 1854; m. 1861
Status: LC; NLI (mf); Indexed by DLHS (b. 1854-1900; m. 1865-1900)

76 Civil Parish of Tully
RC Parish: See Monkstown; also part Taney (1)

21 Civil Parish of Ward
RC Parish: see Finglas

13 Civil Parish of Westpalstown
RC Parish: see Ballyboghill

72 Civil Parish of Whitechurch
RC Parish: see Rathfarnham(1)

Fr. Merritt's R C Register
A further useful source is the register of a Fr. Michael Thomas Merritt
who recorded baptisms and marriages at which he attended from 1800 to
1805 on the northside of Dublin City. Published in the *Irish Genealogist*
Baptisms:
Ir. Gen. 1(4) 1938 pp103-109; 1(5) 1939 pp138-146; 1(6) 1939 pp 171-173
Marriages:
Ir. Gen, 1(7) 1940 pp 208-209; 1(8) 1940 pp 228-236.

YEAR 1842

MOLLOY, Bridget . January 11
MADDEN, Mary . 7 FEBRUARY 18
McDANIEL, Catherine ———— 25
MORAN, Margaret , MARCH 6
MADDEN, Sarah , APRIL 1
MAUD , Jeremiah , APRIL 3
McMAHON, Patrick , ———— 18
MALLON, Michael ———— 26
MURRAY, Peter ———— 30
MORGAN, Christoph. MAY 1
McNALLY, James ———— 5
McCANNA, Christopher ———— 24
McKENNA, John ———— 30
McARDLE, Richard JUNE 5
MEALY, John ———— 19
McCANN, James ———— 19
McNALLY, John ———— 24
MURPHY, John JULY 3
MAGRANE, Catherine ———— 10
McMAHON, Mary ———— 29
McEVOY, Patrick , Septem. 13
MAGRANE, Margaret October 16
McAULEY, Peter , OCTOBER 18
MORGAN, Alice ———— 18
McGLUE, Peter ———— 21
McNALLY, Elizabeth ———— 21
McDANIEL, Catherine , Decemb. 14
McKENNA, Patrick ———— 20

YEAR 1843

MAGENNIS, John , January 23
MULHALL, Mary — February 24

*Some parish registers provide a convenient index
which can be of great assistance to the researcher.
The above marriage index is from the
Roman Catholic parish of Swords.*

Catholic Parish Histories

A series of *Short Histories of Dublin Parishes* written by the Most Rev. Nicholas Donnelly (1837-1920) D.D., Lord Bishop of Canea, Crete, was published by the Catholic Truth Society of Ireland (c.1905 -1917). Below is the complete list of parishes in the series.

Parish	Part(s)	Parish	Part(s)
Arran Quay	X	Howth	XV
Aughrim Street	X	James Street	IX
Balbriggan	XVI	Killiney	V
Baldoyle	XV	Kilmacud	III
Berkeley Street	XI	Kingstown	IV
Blackrock	III	Little Bray	V
Booterstown	III	Lusk	XVI
Cabinteely	V	Marlborough Street	XII/XIII
City Quay	VII	Meath Street	IX
Clontarf	XIV	Monkstown	IV
Coolock	XIV	Naul	XVII
Cullenswood	VI*	North William Street	XII/XIII
Dalkey	IV	Rathgar	VI*
Dolphin's Barn	IX	Rathmines	VI*
Donabate	XV	Ringsend	I/II
Donnybrook	I/II	Rollestown	XVII
Drumcondra	XI	Sandyford	V
Dundrum	III	Sandymount	I/II
Fairview	XIV	Seville Place	XII/XIII
Finglas	XVII	Skerries	XVI
Francis Street	VI*	St. Audeon	VIII
Garristown	XVII	St. Kevin's	VI*
Glasnevin	XIV	St. Michael	VIII
Glasthule	IV	St. Nicholas Without	VI*
Glencullen	V	Stillorgan	III
Haddington Road	I/II	Swords	XV
Halston Street	XI	Westland Row	VII

* part six was published in three separate sections.

— 1822 —

January	8	Henry Hoskins & Sara McGuire
Jan	20	Patrick Lawlor & Charlotte Delany
Jan	20	Francis McGawren & Miss Francis Montomory
Jan	21	Hugh McKelop & Mary Anne Cook
Jan	21	Walter Coleman & Anne Blakemore
Jan	25	William McDermot & Sluny Goughir
Jan.	28	Michael Byrne & Isabele Forsyth
Feb	10	James Willett & Anne Wetherelle
Feb.	10	Laurence Lennax & Sally Lennex
Feb	10	Charles Hare & Mary Anne M Dowd
Feb	11	Mr William Brown & Miss Deborah Martin
Feb	18	Mr James Mackiln & Miss Mary Collins
Feb	23	Samuel Nicolson & Sara Ellis
March	10	Edward Henry Murphy and Jane Drury
March	14	Josia Bridwell & Grace Athn
March	17	Edward Kelsy & Rachel Maridith
March	9	John Brown & Elizabeth Crawley
March	20	Mr Hubert B. Kelly & Miss Hannah Baly
March	24	Saml. Russell & Ellen Miller
March	29	James Dowsy & Ellenor Fee
April	3	Richard Meades & Elisabeth Cuthbert

Marriages entries from 'Irregular Marriages in Dublin before 1837'
- see below

Lutheran Church

A Lutheran church existed in Dublin from about 1697, and it was located in Poolbeg Street from 1725. From 1806 to 1837 the minister, Rev. J.G. Schulze conducted marriage ceremonies (and a few baptisms) on behalf of couples of any denomination. Many of these were eloping couples. These 4,000 marriages were unwitnessed but were subsequently declared valid in court proceedings. The records are held in the GRO and have been published as *'Irregular Marriages in Dublin before 1837'* with a foreword by Dr. R.B. McDowell (Dundalgan Press 2015).

Society of Friends (Quaker Community)

The Society of Friends or Quaker communities maintained excellent records of births, marriages, deaths, obituaries and transfers etc. A full account is given in *'Irish Church Records'* (Flyleaf Press, Dublin, 2001). Most of the records of the Dublin community or meeting are maintained at the Friends Historical Library, in Dublin (see p.153). All records are available for research at this facility and many are available on FMP. The major records are:

Marriage Register: States usual information, plus names of parents. Also indexed are 1812-1848 records: NAI PRO 1047/3/5

Birth Notices: Name of child, parents, birthdate, address (in some cases) and witnesses. Also indexed are 1773 -1943 records in the NAI (PRO1047/3/1 to PRO1047/3/4)

Burial Notices: Name; date of death and burial; location of burial and (in some cases) address. Also indexed are 1779-1912 records in the NAI (1779-1811: NAI PRO1047/3/1; 1824-1840 NAI PRO1047/3/6; 1840-1878 NAI PRO1047/3/7; 1878-1912 NAI PRO1047/3/8

Note also *'A Biographical Dictionary of Irish Quakers'* by Richard S. Harrison (Dublin 2008) and *'The Annual Monitor'* which publishes death notices of all Quakers in Ireland and Britain between 1813-1918.

Jewish Records

The first Jewish immigrants into Ireland arrived from Portugal in the late 17th century. Since then several other groups of Jewish immigrants have arrived from different places. Birth and death records prior to 1870 are held in the Irish Jewish Museum in Dublin at http://jewishmuseum. ie/ There are two useful accounts the Jewish congregation available: (a) Louis Hyman, *A History of the Jews in Ireland* (London/Jerusalem 1972) which includes births from 1820 - 1879, deaths from 1842-1879 and Ballybough Cemetery Inscriptions. (b) B. Schillman, *A Short History of Jews in Ireland* (Dublin 1945).

Street and Commercial Directories can be a useful tool in family history research. The is a good selection of directories for Dublin, both in hard copy and digitally online.

Chapter 6   Commercial and Social Directories

Dublin has a particularly good selection of Commercial Directories. These are privately produced guides to the professions, traders, public servants and gentry in particular areas. An excellent annual series exists from the mid-18th century, and for some of the 19th century there were several competitor directories in publication at the same time. The early directories provide details only on traders and professionals, while the later directories (particularly Thom's) list householders. Good collections are held by NLI, DCLA and NAI and they are increasingly available free on various sites such as Googlebooks, search by the title of the directories listed below.

1738.
Directory of Dublin. A list of approx 3,000 individuals, compiled from 18th century manuscripts uncovered in the reconstruction of Green Street Courthouse. DCPL 2000.

1751-1753
Wilson's Alphabetical List of Names and Places of Abode of the Merchants and Traders of the City of Dublin. 1752/1753 editions were supplements to *Gentleman's and Citizen's Almanac.* - see 1755.

1755
Wilson's Directory of Merchants and Traders is included in *Gentleman's and Citizens Almanac.* (renamed the *Treble Almanac* in 1787). Lists of lawyers, medical practitioners, city officials, clergy and city guild officers were also added. A list of nobility and gentry was added in 1815 and it was gradually enlarged from then on. Issued annually to 1837. The editions for 1783, 1812, 1818 and 1829 are on FMP.

1798
Merchants and Traders of Dublin. Sheila Martin, Genealogical Society of Ireland. Over 4,800 merchants and traders are listed in this publication, the names of which were extracted from "The Gentleman's and Citizen's Almanack" (see above).

1803
Wilson's Dublin Directory. (see 1755) Available online at www.irishancestors.ie

1820

J. Pigot's Commercial Directory of Ireland contains information on the gentry, nobility, and traders in and around Dublin.

1824

J. Pigot's City of Dublin and Hibernian Provincial Directory includes traders, nobility, gentry, and clergy lists for Dublin, Howth, Lucan, and Swords. Available on FMP.

1834

Pettigrew and Oulton's Dublin Almanac and General Register of Ireland has lists of merchants and traders and a list of residents on the main streets. The residents of rented houses were generally not listed, these premises being referred to as tenements. The scope of the directory was gradually increased over the years to include the suburbs. Issued annually to 1849. Some available on FMP.

1843

Post Office Annual Directory and Calendar lists nobility, merchants, professions etc. John S. Fields, Dublin. Available on FMP.

1844 -

Alexander Thom's Irish Almanac and Official Directory has the same categories of lists as Pettigrew and Oulton. It expanded annually to include Dublin suburbs, up to recent times. Some are on FMP

1846

Slater's National Commercial Directory of Ireland lists nobility, clergy, traders, etc., in Balbriggan and Skerries, Blackrock, Booterstown, Dalkey, Dublin, Howth, Kingstown (Dun Laoghaire), Monkstown, Swords, Malahide, and Williamstown. Available on FMP.

1847

Dublin Almanac and General Register of Ireland, lists public official traders and residents of Dublin City and surrounding suburbs. Available on https://books.google.ie/ - see page 87.

1850

Dublin Pictorial Guide and Directory of 1850 (reprint by Friar's Bush Press, 1988) originally published in 1850 by Henry Shaw as *New City Pictorial Directory*. It lists residents, traders by street and surname. It also includes numerous drawings of the main streets. - See page 84.

HAROLD'S CROSS.

Bergan place,
Michael Doyle, lime works
1 Mr. Richard Bennett
2 Mrs. O'Flaherty
3 Marcus Trotter, English and
  writing master
4 Mrs. Ledson
5 Mr. Richard Gordon

Clarke's Buildings,
1 Mrs. Kennedy
2 Mr. Joseph Hogg
3 Mrs. Walsh
4 Mr. John Frederick Meyers
5 Mr. Edward Mayer, and 9
  Temple bar

Elmville Cottages,
1 Mr. Edward M'Donnell, and
  24 New row, West
2 Mr. Michael Martin
3 Mrs. Mitchell
4 Mr. Robert Dark

Harold's cross,
Mr.JosephButler,Jessamine cot.
Richard Sutton, esq. Greenfield
James Sutton, esq.   do
8 Mrs. Finch
9 Mr. John Kathrens
10 John Wardell, grocer, prov.
  dealer, and linen draper
11 Mr. James Eves
„ Jane Eves, haberdasher
12 Mrs. Daly, Greenmount view
Wm. Daly, esq.   do
Female Orphan House & Convent—
  superioress, Mrs. Young;
  Mrs. Murray, mistress
Mr. John M'Coy. Rose villa
Mr. Michael McLaine, do
17 Mr. James Enright, and 40
  Stephen street
18 & 19 Fern. Maximo, saddler
20 Mrs. Emma Parker
„ Mr. John Henry Parker
22 Mr. James Frederick Wilson

30 Mr. Francis Whittaker
31 Mr. Samuel Jackson
32 Mr. John Collier
33 Mrs. Quintin
„ Rev. James Quintin
34 Mrs. Grant
35 Mark Dunn, grocer, spirit
  and provision dealer
38 Mr. Bartholomew Clinch
39 Mrs. O'Hanlon
40 Mr. Patrick O'Moore
41 Mr. Thomas P. Lowe
The Misses Taylor
Philip Meadows Taylor, esq
John McLaine, nurseryman
James Cullen, baker
Mrs. Gibton, Mount Harold
John H. Evans, esq.   do
Mrs. Hughes, Ellenea villa
The Misses Archbold, Souvenir
  cottage
Mr. John Conolly, Cruz del
  Campo
Mr. Thos. M'Conry, Laburnam
John Keatinge, solicitor, Tivoli
  terrace—office, 37 Cuffe street
Miss Curran, Tivoli terrace
Mr. John Freeman, Abbey view
Jas. H. Monks, M.D. accoucheur
„ and apothecary, Terrace
Mrs Byrne,   do
Mr. Peter M'Donogh, Terrace
Mrs. Monks
Joseph Murphy & Son, flour mls.
Peter Murphy, esq
Loader's park paper mills—
  warehouse, 18 Wellington qy.
James Kavanagh, market
  gardener, Rath Land
*Harold's Cross Church,*Rev.Robt.
  J. M'Ghee, chaplain
The Dublin General Cemetry,
  Mount Jerome—chaplain, Rev.
  James Quintin; Mr. Chas. B.
  Johnston, Secretary
Harold's Cross National Free
  Schools

Mr. Thomas Darby
Mr. James Morrin
Miss Whelan
Mr. Alexander Gordon, Green
  Mount terrace
Mr. Charles Cameron, Green
  Mount terrace
James Hanlon, carpt. & builder
Mr. Patrick Quinn, Hollymount,
  and 41 Cork street
Rev. Simpson Gabriel Morrison
Mr. William Harrison
Mrs. Archbold
Mrs. Bennett
Monastery and Mercantile aca-
  demy, Mr. James Murphy,
  superintendent
Mr. Thomas Clarke
Mrs. Aikenhead, St. Mary's Mt.
Greenmount Spinning Company,
  Jonathan Pim, actuary
Mrs. MacMichael, Greenmt-cot.

Kimmage road.
Mrs. Mary Anne Murphy, Roy-
  mount cottage
Mr. Loughlin Doyle
Laurence Murray, esq. Sion hill
John Warham, esq.   do
Mrs. Byrne, Mount Argus
Mr. Samuel Parke
Francis Tuite, Larkfield mills
Mr. James Hyland, Brooklawn
John Flynn, Kimmage mills, &
  Rathmines
Edmund Davy,esq. Kimmage k.
Rev. Henry Stannard, Wains-
  worth
James Bennett, esq. and 8 Aun-
  gier street
Right Hon. Frederick Shaw,LL.S.
  M.P. Recorder of Dublin, Kim-
  mage house
Robt. Shaw,jun. esq. Kimmageh.

Longford row,
1 Mr. John Henry Cunningham

Harold's Cross traders and residents from
Dublin Almanac and General Register of Ireland 1847.

1856

Slater's Royal National Commercial Directory of Ireland lists nobility, gentry, clergy, traders, etc., in Balbriggan and Skerries, Dublin and Kingstown (Dun Laoghaire), Howth, Swords, and Malahide.

1867

Kingstown Directory or Local Guide of Kingstown (Dún Laoghaire), Monkstown, Dalkey and Killiney. (residents, streets, statistics etc.). Download at https://archive.org/details/1867MullanysKingstown

1867

A brief history of Dalkey, with an alphabetical listing of residents and addresses. Jnl. Dun Laoghaire Genealogical Society Vol.7 No.3 p.99 - 110.

1870

Slater's Directory of Ireland contains trade, nobility, and clergy lists for Balbriggan and Skerries, Dalkey, Dublin, Dundrum, Howth, Rathfarnham, Swords, and Malahide.

1872-3

Anderson's Kingstown and Bray Directory, including Dalkey, Killiney, Ballybrack, Monkstown, Blackrock, Booterstown, and Williamstown, with a complete postal guide for each. (First edition in DCLA).

1881

Slater's Royal National Commercial Directory of Ireland lists traders, clergy, nobility and farmers in the parishes of Balbriggan, Skerries, Donabate, Malahide, Dublin, Howth, Baldoyle, Rathfarnham and Swords. Available on FMP

1890

Kingstown Directory (includes Kingstown, Monkstown, Ballybrack, Dalkey and Killiney). Pub. Talbot Coall & Son.

1894

Slater's Royal National Directory of Ireland lists traders, police, teachers, farmers and private residents in Dublin city along with each of the towns, villages and parishes of Dublin county.

1905

Kingstown Directory (includes Kingstown, Monkstown, Dalkey, Killiney and Ballybrack). Pub. Talbot Coall & Son.

1911

Porter's Post Office Guide and Directory of Kingstown, Blackrock, Killiney and Neighbourhood. Includes residents and their occupations.

1912

Porter's Post Office Guide and Directory for North County Dublin Gives occupation of head of households in Artane, Balbriggan, Baldoyle, Blanchardstown, Castleknock, Chapelizod, Clondalkin, Clontarf, Coolock, Donabate, Donnycarney, Dollymount, Drumcondra, Finglas, Fairview, Garristown, Glasnevin, Howth, Inchicore, Kilbarrack, Lucan, Lusk, Malahide, Mulhuddart, Phoenix Park, Portmarnock, Raheny, Rathfarnham, Rush, Skerries and Swords).

TALBOT COALL & SON,

EDEN PARK Glasthule	
1 Owen, Mrs.	4 Ryan, Patrick J., spirit grocer
2 Bate, E. R.	5 Kenney, Mrs.
3 Anderson, F. W.	6 Whelan, T.
4 Byrne, Mrs. K.	9 Millar, M.
5 Benson, Rev. E. M.	10 Mason, F. C., Vet. Surgeon
6 Riordan, E. J.	11 Conroy, John
7 O'Brien, R.A.	12 Reilly Mrs.
8 Ryan, Mrs. E. M.	13 Walsh, P. J.
9 Power Mrs. C.	14 Conway, Michael
10 Galbraith, Mrs.	15 Paynter, Mrs.
11 O'Connor, Mrs.	16 Williams, Miss
12 Le Clerc, Mrs.	17 May, F. H.
13 Jameson, Col. J. R.	18 Smith, Mrs.
	Valetta House—**Browett, F., Nurseries**
EGLINTON PARK Corrig Road	18A Farrell, Mrs.
	Carnegie Library
Burgess, Henry G., Eglinton House	24 Swan, John, tinsmith
1 Beamish, Col. D., U.D.C.	25 Hender, James, dairy
2 Handy, Misses	26 Vacant
3 Posnett, Prof. H. M., LL.D.	27 Vacant
4 Vac., Agts., Talbot Coall & Son	28 Murray, Mrs.
5 Tisdall, E.	30 Young, David, chimney cleaner
6 Vac., Agts. Talbot Coall & Son	St. Mary's Convent
7 Corkery, H.	31 Mulderry, Wm., draper
8 Inman, C. A.	32 Cassidy, Mrs., hairdresser
Spencer Hill—Hickson, Dr. R., R.N.	33 Healy, M.
9 Slevin, T. F.	35 Irish Transport Workers' Union
10 Inman, Col. A.	35A McMullen Bros., victuallers
Eglinton Cottage—Egan, S.	38 Byrne, Mrs., fish dealer
	39 Fox, Robert, hairdresser
	40 Reilly, J., harness maker
	41 Giblin, John, spirit dealer
	42 Burnett, J., chemist
	43 Smith and Barton, stationers

1913
A directory of Kingstown (Monkstown, Dalkey, Killiney) and district published by Talbot Coall and Son. Includes historical notes, photographs with a detailed map showing streets and houses. Download available at http://www.swilson.info/kingstown1913.php?img=1 - see above.

Biographical Dictionaries:

1600-1720
A Biographical Dictionary of Architects in Ireland 1600-1720
Loeber, Rolf. Murray 1981.

1816-1922
Royal Irish Constabulary Officers (A complete alphabetical list of officers and men) Herlihy, Jim. Dublin: Four Courts Press 2005.

1834-1934
The Irish County Surveyors 1834-1934. O'Donoghue, Brendan.
Dublin: Four Courts 2007

1836-1925

*Dublin Metropolitan Police (*A complete alphabetical list of officers and men) Herlihy, Jim. Dublin: Four Courts Press 2001.

1908

Dublin and County Dublin in the 20th Century - Contemporary Biographies. (includes portrait of each).
Cosgrave, MacDowel and Pike (Eds). Brighton and London 1908.

1916-1923

Who's Who in the Irish War of Independence and Civil War 1916-1923.
O'Farrell, Padraic. Dublin: Lilliput 1997.

1914 -

The Pals at Suvla Bay is a record of 'D' Company of the 7th Royal Dublin Fusiliers by Henry Hannah (1916) It includes brief biographies of its members with head and shoulder photos for most of them. See extract below. Available from www.naval-military-press.com/

O'NEILL, CHARLES

Born at Dollymount, Co. Dublin. Son of H. G. O'Neill, of Dublin. Educated at Clontarf and privately. Clerk, Bank of Ireland. Gun-shot wound in right thigh and dysentery, August 22, 1915. Invalided two days later. One of the reserves landed at Mudros who rejoined Battalion, August 16, 1915. Now Corporal, attached to 10th Battalion Royal Dublin Fusiliers.

PARRY, STANLEY KAYE

Born at Kingstown, Co. Dublin. Son of W. Kaye Parry. Educated at Trent College, Derbyshire, and Trinity College, Dublin. B.A. (Trinity College, Dublin). Chartered Accountant. Made Lance-Corporal, January 1915, and Corporal a week later; Lance-Sergeant, August 1915. Gazetted Second Lieutenant 7th Royal Dublin Fusiliers, September 1915.

O'SULLIVAN, GARTH R.

Born at Dublin. Son of the late Dr. J. A. O'Sullivan, of Ballsbridge, Co. Dublin. Educated at St. Vincent's College, Castleknock. Apprentice, Mercantile Marine (Lord Line). Invalided, suffering from dysentery, August 1915. Gazetted Second Lieutenant 6th Royal Irish Rifles, December 1915.

PAUL, CHARLES A.

Born at Dublin. Son of C. J. Paul, of Dublin. Educated at Howth Road and Wesley College, Dublin. Insurance Clerk. Made Lance-Corporal, August 1915. Invalided, suffering from dysentery, August 24, 1915. Gazetted Second Lieutenant 6th Royal Dublin Fusiliers, December 1915. Now serving at Salonika.

1923

Thom's Who's Who. Contains biographical accounts of over 2,500 Irish men and women, residing in Ireland and abroad. This first edition, published by Alexander Thom in 1923 is available on CD from Archive CD books at www.archivecdbooks.ie

Chapter 7   Wills and Administrations

A Will is the written instructions of a deceased person as to the division of their assets after their death. The maker of the will (the testator) will usually specify the distribution of the property, and appoint a trusted person (the Executor) to carry out their instructions. To achieve a legal status, a will must be accepted, or 'proven' by a Probate court.

If a deceased person died without making a will (i.e. intestate), the court must decide on the distribution of assets on their behalf, taking account of their family and creditor situation. This is called an administration. On certain occasions where a will has been made but it is inoperable (e.g. the executor is also deceased) an administration may also be made.

The court appointed Administrator is usually a relative or legal person, whose task is to oversee the distribution of the estate of the deceased as determined by the court. The Administrator enters a bond for a sum of money as a surety that the instructions of the court will be carried out. These bonds are called Administration Bonds.

Wills and administrations can provide the researcher with excellent information on family relationships. The details can sometimes resemble a brief family pedigree. The Probate records available to researchers are as follows:

Original Wills and Administrations: These are potentially important legal documents with a particular relevance in proving ownership of property. They are stored in many different archives, as well as in private collections. The major collection of Irish wills was unfortunately destroyed in the Public Record Office fire in 1922.

Name, Place, and Occupation.	Year.	Nature of Record.	Page.
Kells, George and Sarah Hepburn, .	1752	M.L.	224
Kellshy, Richard, St. Michan's, Dublin,	1679	W.	**51
Kelly, Abigail, Dublin,	1716	I.	34
„ Alice and Hugh Alexander, .	1794	M.L.	8
„ Alice and Humphrey Walley, .	1661	M.L.	11
„ Anastace (alias Tommins), Jodines, co. Kild., widow, .	1729	W.	*203
„ Andrew, Blackrath, co. Kild.,	1783	I.	67
„ Ann (alias Lewis), Francis-st., widow,	1636	O.W	—
„ Ann (alias French), Dublin, .	1762	I.	352
„ Ann, Dublin, widow, .	1772	W.	91
„ Ann and Cornelius Callaghan,	1782	M.L.	24
„ Ann and John Burroughs,	1753	M L	258
„ Ann and Robert Donovan,	1759	M.L.	125
„ Ann and Thomas James,	1778	M.L.	224
„ Ann and George Kelly,	1792	M.L.	284
„ Ann and Robert Owen,	1757	M.L.	492
„ Ann and Ebenezer Ralph,	1792	M.L.	284
„ Anne, Chequer-lane, .	1686	I.	**230
„ Anne and Henry Cochran,	1789	M.L.	41
„ Anne and John Lyster,	1791	M.L.	152
„ Anthony, Patrick-st., tobacconist, .	1775	I.	221
„ Anthony and Ann Webb,	1790	M.L.	113
„ Bartholomew, Drumcondra-lane, .	1768	I.	414
„ Bernard, .	1704	I.	**147
„ Bernard, Dublin, surgeon, .	1769	I.	555
„ Bernard, Dorset-st., servant,	1794	W.	57
„ Bridget and Thomas Hautenville,	1799	M.L.	483
„ Bryan, Dolphin's Barn, co. Dub.,	1778	I.	228
„ Catherine, Meath-st., .	1748	W.	476
„ Catherine, Dublin, spinster, .	1763	I.	420
„ Catherine, Francis-st., spinster,	1789	I.	30
„ Catherine and John Broughall,	1773	M.L.	125
„ Catherine and Francis Poole,	1759	M.L.	85
„ Catherine and Edward Rice,	1772	M.L.	80
„ Catherine and Thomas Stokes,	1799	M.L.	428
„ Charles, Dublin, joiner,	1754	I.	311
„ Charles and Eliza Hutchison,	1799	M.L.	478
„ Charles Aylmer, Clarendon-st.,	1795	W.	105
„ Charles Aylmer and Pruella (Precilla in Bond) Hutton,	1784	M.L.	131
„ Christopher, .	1775	W.	212
„ Christopher, Church-st., yeoman, .	1734	I.	276
„ Christopher, Vicar-st., cheesemonger,	1775	W.	21
„ Cordelia, Dublin, widow, .	1772	W.	91
„ Cornelius, Ardmore, farmer,	1731	I.	234

A page from the '26th Report of the Deputy Keeper of the Public Records and Keeper of State Papers in Ireland' which consisted of an index to original Wills at the Diocese of Dublin to 1800. - see page 97

Abstracts: For various legal and family history purposes, details of the persons and properties mentioned in certain wills have been abstracted and either published or otherwise made available for consultation.

Indexes: Although a large proportion of Irish wills have been destroyed, the index to some collections survive and provide name, residence and date of death of each testator. Indexes for existing wills obviously also survive, and are usefully detailed.

Pre-1858 Wills and Administrations

Prior to 1858 Probate administration was the responsibility of the Church of Ireland, and all wills were proven in either the Prerogative court in Armagh, or a Diocesan (or Consistorial) court in each diocese.

The Prerogative Court (The Prerogative Court of the Archbishop of Armagh) was responsible for the proving of wills of a person whose property lay within two or more dioceses where the value in the second diocese was £5 or more. Such wills were generally made by more wealthy individuals. However, landholders whose property straddled the border of two dioceses may also be included. All Prerogative wills and grants in the PRO were destroyed in the 1922 fire. However, some replacement material has been obtained and is in the NAI.

Surviving Records:
Will Books: All were destroyed except those proved from 1664-84 and 1706-08 for those with surnames beginning with A-W; and 1726-29 (also Surnames A-W); 1777 (A-L); 1813 (K-Z); 1834 (A - E). Copies of the above Wills and Will Book entries, are indexed in the Testamentary Card index in the NAI.

Will Indexes to Prerogative Wills survive and are arranged alphabetically by surname giving testator's address, occupation and year of probate.
(a) An index for the period 1536-1810, edited by Sir Arthur Vicars, was published as *'Index to the Prerogative Wills of Ireland'* (Dublin 1897). It is available on FMP. The manuscript index is available in the NAI.
(b) The manuscript index for 1811-1857 is in the NAI.
(c) *'Irish Wills and Testaments in Great Britain 1600-1700'* by David Dobson (1996). These include English or Scottish settlers in Ireland and residents of Ireland who died in the service of the British Crown or aboard English ships. Copy in NLI.

An extract from 'Index to the Prerogative Wills of Ireland 1536-1810'
edited by Sir Arthur Vicars(Dublin 1897)

Will and Grant Abstracts: Betham's pre-1802 Abstracts (i.e. notes on family information extracted from wills and grants) are in the NAI and Betham's sketch pedigrees (constructed from the above abstracts) are in the GO.

Grants: Indexes to grants for 1595-1858 in NAI and available on FMP. Also Grant Books exist for the period (1684-88; 1748-51; 1839).

Prerogative Day-books: for the period 1748-88, in the NAI.

The Diocesan, or Consistorial, Court was responsible for the proving of wills of persons whose property lay within one diocese. All of County Dublin lies in the CoI Diocese of Dublin, for which the following records survive:

Wills: All surviving wills are indexed in the Testamentary Card index in the NAI.

Will Indexes:
(a) Dublin and Glendalough (1536-1858) published in the appendices to the 26th and 30th reports of the DKPRI of 1895 and 1899 respectively, available on FMP.
(b) *Register of Wills and Inventories of the Diocese of Dublin 1457-1483* by Henry F. Berry: Dublin 1898.

Will Abstracts for the period 1560-1710 (for surnames A - E) are in the GO Ms 290. The Lane-Poole Papers contain 52 will abstracts of 17 to 19th c. from Dublin and Wicklow. These are in NLI (ms. 5359) and also published in Ir. Gen. Vol. 8 (4) 1993 p 610-617.

Grants: Indexes to Administration bonds for 1638-1858 are published in the appendices to the 26th and 30th reports of the DKPRI of 1895 and 1899 respectively. Copies of surviving bonds are also in the Testamentary Card index in the NAI.

Post-1858 Wills and Administrations

Following the abolition of the Ecclesiastical Courts (Prerogative and Diocesan) in 1857, a civil court system was established. It comprised a Principal Registry and eleven District Registries. The Principal Registry effectively replaced the Prerogative Court. The District Registries replaced the Diocesan Courts. Dublin wills are proved in the Principal Registry. The surviving records are kept in the NAI and a searchable index (or 'Calendar') for the years from 1858-1920 is available on-line at http://www.willcalendars.nationalarchives.ie/search/cwa/index.jsp and full calendars of wills from 1922 to 1982 can be down loaded in pdf format from http://nai.adlibhosting.com/results While the original will my not survive, these indexes provide useful information. - see page 96.

Other Will and Abstract collections include:

The Genealogical Office, Dublin, published by the Irish Manuscripts Commission 1998.This publication contains an index to Will abstracts in the Genealogical Office, part of the National Library of Ireland. It provides the names, addresses (location), date and place of probate. An occupation is given in many entries.

BUSSELL Henry.	8 June.	The Will
[172] Effects £490.	of Henry Bussell late of 2 Willow-terrace Williamstown County **Dublin** Gentleman deceased who died 3 April 1882 at same place was proved at the **Principal Registry** by Sidney P. Bussell of Dalkey in said County and of 24 Dame-street Dublin Solicitor the sole Executor.	
BUTLER Alice.	7 July.	Letters of Administration
[200] Effects £192 17s. 10d.	of the personal estate of Alice Butler late of 55 Watling-street **Dublin** deceased who died 10 April 1882 at same place were granted at the **Principal Registry** to John Butler of 55 Watling-street Gentleman the Husband.	
BUTLER Anne.	13 March.	Letters of Administration
[79] Effects £11,976 12s. 2d.	of the personal estate of Anne Butler formerly of Sandymount County Dublin and late of Rue de Chateaubriand Paris in **France** Spinster deceased who died 6 January 1882 at latter place were granted at the **Principal Registry** to Walter Butler of Rue d' Ermitage Versailles in France Esquire the Brother.	

Entries from the 1882 'Calendar of Wills and Administrations'.
They can provide basic but useful information in the absence of an original will.

World War 1 Irish Soldiers: Their Final Testament. The wills of 9,000 Irishmen in the British armed forces who died during the conflict 1914-1918. The contents include names, addresses of next of kin and various other details in the case of each soldier. A search facility and pdf downloads of the wills is accessable from http://soldierswills. nationalarchives.ie/search/sw/home.jsp

Quaker Wills from Dublin and East Leinster. Society of Friends Library, Dublin. - See page 150.

Banns and Marriage Licenses

Two methods were available to churches to ensure against an impediment to a marriage. The first was the Banns, which involved reading, or posting the names of a couple about to marry. These effectively gave three weeks public notice of the impending marriage so any objections could be made. Banns were read in the parish church of each of the marrying couple and in the church in which the marriage would take place, if the couple were marrying elsewhere. For some reason, marriage by Banns was regarded as an indication of poverty by many and was avoided by most couples. Usually, a fee would be paid to the Church of Ireland minister to have the Banns waived. The alternative, a Marriage License was obtained (prior to 1858), from the Ecclesiastical courts noted above. It involved a payment (a surety) to indemnify the church against any damages that may be sought later as a result of any unforeseen impediment to the marriage. These sureties were called Marriage Licence Bonds.

Two types of marriage licences were issued:
(a) Diocesan Marriage Licences which were valid for three months and allowed the couple to marry within the diocese.

(b) Prerogative Marriage Licences were issued by the Prerogative Court of Armagh and allowed the couple to marry anywhere with no time restrictions.

Marriage Licence Bonds Indexes are available as follows:

Prerogative Marriage Licence Bonds Indexes (1629-1858) NLI GO Ms. 605-687.

Prerogative Marriage Licence Bonds Indexes (1750-1861) NAI (Open Access). .
Indexes to Dublin Diocesan Bonds (1672-1741) NAI (Open access).

Original Diocesan Bonds, Dublin (1749-1813) indexed by males, surnames beginning with A only. NAI ; SLC 101770 Also Dublin Grant Book and Wills etc (1270-1858).

Abstracts. Fisher's Abstracts (1638-1800), indexed separately for bride and groom, by surname, gives groom's name, address, bride's name and address, and date of marriage: GO MS 134-38; SLC Film 100226

Listing of Dublin ML abstracts (1638-1800). Phillip's listing, by both bride and grooms' surnames of all marriage licenses granted, and intended place of marriage. GO MS 473-75.

The 26th and 30th Reports of the DKPRI also indexes marriage licenses for the Dublin and Glendalough diocese. - See page 92.

KILTERNAN

KILTERNAN C.O.I.:- Located in Kilternan Village. The church, which has a very active community, was built circa 1816. It is surrounded by a well maintained graveyard which has been in use since 1841.

1   Erected by Elizabeth Harding ilm her parents John Harding, d 10/9/1919 age 71yrs, Anne Harding, d 23/4/1916 age 82yrs.

2   Warren Storey MIEE. MICE. (I), d 16/2/1952. Esther Storey, d 20/2/1961.

3   Sidney Howard Guilford, d 28/4/1953, his wife Caroline Edith, d 4/3/1966.

4   Martha Power, d 18/4/1970.

5   Benjamin B Russell, killed in Manx Grand Prix at Lezayre, 9/9/1947. May Elizabeth Russell, d 29/3/1955. George Alexander Russell, d 27/12/1956.

6   James East, formerly of Fort Louis, Sligo, d 23/2/1950. His wife Eleanor, d 22/1/1951, his son J Sidney East of Clonskeagh, Dublin 1911-1991.

7   Arthur Cowan Digby French, Priest 1876-1950. Synolda Georgina, his wife, 1881-1971. Robert Butler Digby French, 1904-1981. Eleanor (Nell) Digby French, 1906-1992.

8   Arthur Joseph Thompson, d 27/11/1951 age 49yrs. His son Alan David, died September 1963 age 17yrs. Frances E Thompson, (nee Mercier), wife of Arthur, d 10/4/1990.

9   Isobel H M Downs, d 19/5/1975. Robert W Downs, d 29/9/1978.

10 Gladys Ross, d 14/9/1990.

11 Agnes Grace (Queenie) Stewart, daughter of Captain and Mrs Hugh Stewart, Hatlex, Foxrock, Co Dublin, died September 1950. Harriet Amy (Harrie), d 4/6/1965. Mary (May) Stewart RRC. OAIMNS., d 30/12/1969 age 94yrs.

12 Frances Jane Hilton (nee Richardson), d 6/1/1952 age 75yrs wife and mother. John Hilton, d 22/3/1956 age 83yrs husband and father.

Memorial inscriptions can be an excellent source for the family historian. The inscriptions of many Dublin graveyards have been published. The above extracts are from Kiltiernan Church of Ireland - see page 104.

Chapter 8   Gravestone Inscriptions

As civil registration of deaths in Ireland only commenced in 1864, and few churches kept burial records, gravestones provide one of the very few pre-1864 sources of information about date and place of death. Many gravestones provide only the name of the deceased and the date of death. However, some are more detailed, and provide excellent biographical details about the deceased, and about other relatives. The graves of poorer persons, unfortunately, were often unmarked, or marked with wooden memorials. Gravestones cannot be expected for poorer ancestors It should be remembered that Catholics, Methodists and Presbyterians may be buried in Church of Ireland graveyards. CoI graveyard and burial records should therefore always be checked, whatever the denomination of the family.

For Dublin, some major sources of Gravestone Inscriptions are:

(a) The series *'Memorials of the Dead - Dublin City and County'* was compiled by Michael T.S. Egan and published by the Irish Genealogical Research Society and Michael T.S. Egan (These are noted below as Mems - Dublin); To date, 10 volumes have been published between 1988 and 1997.

(b) *Journals of the Association for the Preservation of the Memorials of the Dead in Ireland (1888-1921).* The entries are selective, since they were dependent on contributions by individual members. In many cases transcriptions from a specific graveyard were published over several years in various volumes. These usually do not provide a full set of transcripts from each graveyard.

Both of the above are privately published but are available in most major archives and libraries. See also the 'Early Irish Death Index' available from the IGRS (www.irish ancestors.ie)

There are over 200 graveyards in Co. Dublin of which only a fraction have been transcribed and published in some form. However, the burial registers of two of Dublin's larger cemeteries, are available, Deansgrange Cemetery (1865-1972) and Mount Jerome (1836-1972) are on microfilm in the DCLA - page 150. A copy of the Deansgrange registers are on microfilm held by the GSI.

An account of the graveyards of Dublin and the status of their records is given in 'Directory of Graveyards in the Dublin Area - an Index and Guide to Burial Records' Dublin Public Libraries 1990, ISBN 0946841136 also as a database at http://databases.dublincity.ie/graveyards/
Local genealogical and historical societies continue to transcribe and publish complete surveys of graveyards. Local journals should therefore be checked for new additions. Some of these publications may be difficult to find. A useful source is Google books.

Inscriptions published or otherwise available to date:

Abbotstown:
Ir. Gen. 6 (6) 1985 pp 824-827; & 7(1) 1986, pp. 124-128; also MEMS: Dublin Vol. 3.
Aderrig:
J. Assoc. Pres. Mem. Dead. X, p. 191 and J.Ir. Mem. Assoc. XI, p.155.
Arbour Hill:
Arbour Hill Military Cemetery – Memorials of Military Personnel and their Families Stationed in Ireland (CD) GSI 2009.
Ardla:
Indexed by Swords Hist Soc. see p.152.
Artane:
(1100's-1700): J. Ir. Mem. Assoc. XI, p.409-413.
Balbriggan (St. George's):
J. Ass. Pres. Mem. Dead. iii, p.62-64; viii, p.277; and MEMS: Dublin Vol. 6.
Baldungan
MEMS: Dublin Vol. 9.
Balgriffin - see St. Doolough's
Ballybough (Jewish):
The Jews of Ireland to the Year 1910, Hyman, L. (1972) and *Short History of the Jews of Ireland,* Shillman, B., (1945).
Ballyboughal:
MEMS: Dublin Vol. 6.

Ballymadun:
(1800-): J. Ir. Mem. Assoc. xi, p.217-221; and Mems-Dublin Vol. 5.
Balrothery:
MEMS: Dublin Vol. 6.
Balrothery Union:
MEMS: Dublin Vol. 6.
Balscadden (New and Old):
MEMS: Dublin Vol. 6. Also indexed by Swords Hist Soc. see p.153.
Barringtons Burial Ground:
see Brennanstown.
Blackrock:
Carmelite Monastery - Memorial Inscriptions of Dun Laoghaire Rathdown Vol.3 – GSI (2005). Friends Burial Ground, Temple Hill. - Memorial Inscriptions of Dun Laoghaire Rathdown Vol. 2 – GSI (2003). Sion Hill Convent - Memorial Inscriptions of Dun Laoghaire Rathdown Vol.3 GSI (2005) and Blackrock College: Memorial Inscriptions of Dun Laoghaire Rathdown Vol.1 – GSI (2000). - see also Deansgrange.
Bluebell (Old):
(1713-): MEMS: Dublin Vol. 3.
Bohernabreena:
St. Anne's Old Graveyard. Michael Murphy 1997.
Bremore (Balbriggan):
MEMS: Dublin Vol. 6.
Brennanstown:
Memorial Inscriptions of Dun Laoghaire Rathdown Vol.1 – GSI (2000). also MEMS: Dublin Vol. 9
Bully's Acre:
see Kilmainham.
Cabbage Garden:
see Cathedral Lane
Cabinteely:
see Brennanstown.
Capuchin Burial Ground:
see Cathedral Lane
Carrickbrennan:
see Monkstown.
Cathedral Lane:
Typescript index to tombstones and memorials in DCLA.
Chapelizod:
Ir. Gen. 5 (4) (1977): p.490-505.

Chapelmidway (Kilsallaghan):
MEMS: Dublin Vol. 5, also indexed by Swords Hist Soc. see page 152.
Christ Church Cathedral- Dublin City:
Finlayson, Rev. Inscriptions on the Monuments . . . in Christ Church Cathedral. Dublin, 1878.
Cloghran:
Adams, Rev. Benjamin W. History and Description of Santry and Cloghran Parishes: 1883.
Cloghran:
MEMS: Dublin Vol. 4.
Cloghran-Hidart:
MEMS: Dublin Vol. 4.
Clondalkin (St. John's C of I):
MEMS: Dublin Vol. 8.
Clonmethan (Oldtown):
MEMS: Dublin Vol. 5.
Clonsilla (St Mary's):
Ir. Gen. 6 (5) 1984. pp.680 and MEMS: Dublin Vol. 8.
Colmanstown:
(1743-) MEMS: Dublin Vol. 3.
Cruagh (Rathfarnham):
MEMS: Dublin Vol. 4.
Crumlin (St Mary's CoI):
Ir. Gen. 7(3) 1988 p 454-473 also MEMS: Dublin Vol. 9.
Dalkey (St Begnet's):
Ir. Gen. 5 (2) (1975): p.250-55.
Damastown (Hollywood):
MEMS: Dublin Vol. 5.
Deans Grange (Blackrock): South West Section (Vol. 1, 1994), Lower North Section (Vol. 2, 1997), Upper North Section (Vol. 3 1998), South Section (Vol. 4, 2000) and West Section (Vol. 5, 2002) published by Dun Laoghaire Genealogical Society.
Donabate:
MEMS: Dublin Vol. 8, also indexed by Swords Hist Soc. see page 152.
Donnybrook:
(C.800 - 1993) compiled by Danny Parkinson. pub: 1993 Dublin Family Hist. Soc. 1988.
Dun Laoghaire:
Dominican Convent. Memorial Inscriptions of Dun Laoghaire Rathdown Vol.1 – GSI (2000).

Dundrum:

see Taney

Esker:

Ir. Gen. 6 (1): p.54-58. See extract below.

McKEON: Erected by John McKeon in memory of his ancestors. Also 10 of his children who died young. Also Jams. Korigan depd. this life Augt. 1808 aged 25 years.

MASTERSON: Ledger + This tomb was erected by James Masterson of Ballyowen, Co. Dublin, in memory of his beloved father William Masterson 18th December 1856 aged 80 years. Also his brother Owen died 7th July 1850 aged 25 years. And Thomas died 26th Decer. 1856 aged 47 years. And also Matthew died 2nd Octr. 1857 aged 50 years. Also Laurence who died 16th of Octr. 1858 aged 30 years. And Mrs. Bridget Ledwidge daughter to the above who died 30th July 1860 aged 40 years. Also his mother Mrs Margaret Masterson who died 24th Jan. 1865 aged 90 years. And his sister Mrs. Mary Hall who died 16th Novr. 1867 aged 50 years. And also the above named James Masterson who died 25 Feb. 1870 aged 42 years. Also his daughter Josephine Masterson who died 28th Jan. 1871 aged 6 years.

MERRIMAN: (Lamb) Erected by Thomas and John Merriman in memory of their beloved father Michael Merriman who died January 31st 1879 aged 66 years. Also their beloved mother Anne Merriman who died December 19th 1883 aged 76 years. Also of William eldest son of the above Michael and Anne Merriman who died August 17th 1905 aged 67 years.

MIGGEE: Here lieth the body of John Miggee who departed this life Decer. ye 29th 1773 aged 32 years. Also two of his children.

MURPHY: Of your charity pray for the soul of Miss Mary Murphy late of Clondalkin. She died 14th of February 1849 aged 72 years.

NANGLE: Table Tomb. + IHS Here lyeth the Body of Mr. Patrick Nangle of Church-street, Vintner, who departed this life the 14th December 1788 Aged 34 years. Also here lyeth

Esker (Old), Lucan:

MEMS: Dublin Vol. 2.

Finglas (C. of I.):

J. Ir. Memorials Assoc. (Parish Register Section) 1926-31.

Friends Burial Ground:

see Blackrock.

Garristown:

MEMS: Dublin Vol. 5.

Glencullen (old):

Memorial Inscriptions of Dun Laoghaire Rathdown Vol.1 – GSI (2000).

Glendruid:

See Brennanstown, Cabinteely.

Goldenbridge, Inchicore:

(1829) MEMS: Dublin Vol. 1.

Grallagh, (Naul):

MEMS: Dublin Vol. 5.

Grange, The (Baldoyle):

MEMS: Dublin Vol. 4.

Grangegorman:

Military Cemetery – GSI (2006) See p.105

Hollywood (Naul):

MEMS: Dublin Vol. 6.

Holmpatrick (Skerries):
MEMS: Dublin Vol. 7, also indexed by Swords Hist Soc. see page 152.
Howth Abbey:
MEMS: Dublin Vol. 9.
Huguenot (French): see Peter Street
Inchicore:
see Goldenbridge
Irishtown:
Ir. Gen. Ir. Gen. 7(4) pp. 599-614.
Kenure (Rush):
MEMS: Dublin Vol. 7 and 8, also indexed by Swords Hist Soc. see page 152.
Kilbarrack:
Monumental Inscriptions. NLI Ms. 20, 651 (i) (43 inscriptions)
Kilbride (Baldonnell):
MEMS: Dublin Vol. 2 and Ir. Gen. 6 (3) p.81.
Kilgobbin (New):
MEMS: Dublin Vol. 3.
Kilgobbin (Old):
MEMS: Dublin Vol. 2.
Killeek:
MEMS: Dublin Vol. 5.
Killiney (Old Graveyard):
Ir. Gen. 4 (6) (1973): p.647-48.
Killossery:
MEMS: Dublin Vol. 5, also indexed by Swords Hist Soc. see page 152.
Kilmactalway (Castle Bagot) Baldonnell:
MEMS: Dublin Vol. 2. and Ir. Gen. 6 (3): p.378-81
Kilmahuddrick:
MEMS: Dublin Vol. 2: and Ir. Gen. 6 (3): p.378-81.
Kilmainham, Royal Hospital:
Bully's Acre and Royal Hospital graveyards. History and Inscriptions.
Sean Murphy, Divelina Publications, Dublin 1989. ISBN 9512611 0.
Kilsallaghan:
MEMS: Dublin Vol. 4.
Kilternan Old:
MEMS: Dublin Vol. 2 and Memorial Inscriptions of Dun Laoghaire
Rathdown Vol.1 – GSI (2000).
Kill o' the Grange:
Memorial Inscriptions of Dun Laoghaire Rathdown Vol.3 – GSI (2005)
also Ir. Gen. 4 (5) (1972): p.507-14.

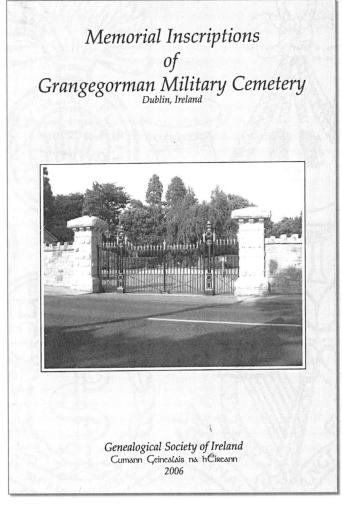

Memorial Inscriptions
of
Grangegorman Military Cemetery
Dublin, Ireland

Genealogical Society of Ireland
Cumann Ƈeinealais na hƐireann
2006

Memorial Inscriptions of Grangegorman Military Cemetery
contains over 1,100 inscriptions including some 800
of British and Commonwealth Service Personnel

Laughanstown:
see Tully.
Leixlip:
Ir. Gen. 4 (2) (1969): p.110-16.
Loughlinstown:
Memorial Inscriptions of Dun Laoghaire Rathdown Vol.1 – GSI (2000).
Loughtown Lower:
Ir. Gen. 6 (3): p.378-81.

Loughtown Lower (Religeen-Newcastle):
MEMS: Dublin Vol. 2.
Lucan:
Ir. Gen. 5 (6) (1976): p.763-67. also St. Mary's: MEMS: Dublin Vol. 2.
Lusk Cof I:
MEMS: Dublin Vol. 8.
Malahide:
MEMS: Dublin Vol. 9, also indexed by Swords Hist Soc. see page 152.
Merrion (Merrion Road):
MEMS: Dublin Vol. 2.
Merrion Row (Huguenot):
MEMS: Dublin Vol. 2.
Milverton:
MEMS: Dublin Vol. 9, also indexed by Swords Hist Soc. see page 152.
Monkstown:
Ir. Gen. 4 (3) (1970): p.201-02; 4 (4) 1971; also pub. by Danny Parkinson.
(Dublin 1988); and Memorial Inscriptions of Dun Laoghaire Rathdown
Vol.3 – GSI (2005).
A list of burials can be found in *Carrickbrennan Graveyard Monkstown,*
Dun Laoghaire Borough Historical Society n.d. - see page 109.
Mount Jerome:
Burial records (1837-1972) on microfilm in the DCLA.
Mount St. Joseph (Clondalkin):
MEMS: Dublin Vol. 2.
Mulhuddart (Old):
MEMS: Dublin Vol. 4, also indexed by Swords Hist Soc. see page 152.
Naul:
MEMS: Dublin Vol. 5.
Newcastle:
Ir. Gen. 6 (2) (1981): p.219-26.
Newcastle (C of I and RC):
MEMS: Dublin Vol. 2.
Old Connaught:
Memorial Inscriptions of Dun Laoghaire Rathdown Vol.1 – GSI (2000).
Palmerstown:
Ir. Gen. 4 (5) (1978): p.650-53.
Palmerstown (Oldtown):
MEMS: Dublin Vol. 4.
Peter Street: 'Peter Street Cemetery-NonConformist French Huguenot
Church...Dublin 1711-1879' by Mona Germaine (Dublin 1999)

Phoenix Park:
Royal Hibernian Military School – Memorials of Military Personnel and their Families Stationed in Ireland (CD) – GSI (2009).
Portmarnock C of I:
MEMS: Dublin Vol. 10 (1997)
Portrane:
MEMS: Dublin Vol. 7 (1994) and Vol. 8 (1995)
Quaker Community - see Blackrock.
Rathcoole:
Ir. Gen. 6 (4) (1983): p.523-25.
Rathcoole (C of I):
MEMS: Dublin Volume 2
Rathfarnham:
Ir. Gen. 7(2) 1987, pp 293-306 - see also Whitechurch.
Rathmichael: Memorial Inscriptions of Dun Laoghaire Rathdown Vol.1 – GSI (2000).
Rolestown:
Indexed by Swords Hist Soc. see p.152.
Royal Hibernian Military:
see Phoenix Park
Royal Hospital Kilmainham:
- see page108.
Rush:
see Whitestown and Kenure.
Saggart:
New 1895 and Old 1711- MEMS: Dublin Vol. 3.
Santry:
Adams, Rev. Benjamin W. History and Description of Santry and Cloghran Parishes. 1883.
St. Anne's: see **Bohernabreena**
St. Andrew's, Westland Row:
Ir. Gen. 5 (1) (1974): 131-39. and NLI Ms. 20.651 (ii) (50 Inscriptions, names on coffin plates).)
St Audoen's:
Published in *'Among the Graves - Inscriptions in St Audoen's Church, Cornmarket, Dublin'* by John Crawford, Dublin 1990.
St. Catherine's:
Memorial Inscriptions from St. Catherine's Church and Graveyard. Sean Murphy. Divelina Publications, 1987
St. Doolough's:
Ir. Gen. 7(1) 1986, pp. 124-128. also MEMS: Dublin Vol. 9

St. James's Graveyard:
Memorial Inscriptions. Published by St. James's Graveyard Project 1988. NAI.

St. Margaret's:
MEMS: Dublin Vol. 9, also indexed by Swords Hist Soc. see p.152.

St. Mary's (Lucan):
MEMS: Dublin Vol. 2.

St. Matthew's (C of I):
MEMS: Dublin Vol. 2.

St. Michael and John:
Names on coffin plates in vaults. Ir. Gen. 5 (3) 1976, pp. 368-9.

St. Patrick's Cathedral:
Monuments in St. Patrick's Cathedral. Victor Jackson (Dublin 1987).

St. Paul (C of I):
R.S.A.I. 104 (1974). p.368-69.

Ss.Peter and John:
Names on coffin plates. Ir. Gen. 5 (3) (1976):

Stillorgan:
St Brigid's CoI. Memorial Inscriptions of Dun Laoghaire Rathdown Vol.1–GSI (2000).

Stoneybatter: see Arbour Hill.

Kilmainham graveyards   26

GORDEN 35
Here lieth the body of George Gorden who depard this
life Decr 23d 1776 aged 65 and two of his [grand?]-
children George & James Gorden. Here also lieth the
body of James Gorden, son of the above, who departed
[thi]s life the 1st of July 1793 aged 37 years.
[Printed in JAPMDI, 9, 1913, 82.]

GREEN 41
IHS with cross. This stone was erected by Mrs Mary
Green to the memory of her beloved husband Mr William
Green late of Anglesea Street, bookseller, who departed
this life Sepr 21st 1808 aged 5?9 years.

HARRINGTON 3
IHS with cross and heart. Here lyeth the body of James
Harrington of Boe Bridge who departed this life the 22
Febr 1786 aged 39 years. Also here lyeth 5 of his

An extract from 'Bully's Acre and Royal Hospital Graveyards' - see page 107

Swords (St Colomba's Col):
In fond remembrance; Inscriptions from St Colomba's Graveyard. pub. Fingal Heritage Group (Dublin 1989). -see Swords Hist Soc - p.152.

Swords (St Colmcille's RC):
Rest in Peace; Inscriptions from St Colmcille's Graveyard. Fingal Heritage Group (Dublin 1989).

Tallaght:
Ir. Gen. 4 (1) (1968): p.29-36.

Taney (St. Nathi's):
The Parish of Taney. by F. E. Ball & E. Hamilton. Dublin 1895

Templeogue (Old):
MEMS: Dublin Vol. 2.

Tully:
Memorial Inscriptions of Dun Laoghaire Rathdown Vol.1 – GSI (2000) also MEMS: Dublin Vol. 9.

The Ward:
MEMS: Dublin Vol. 4, also indexed by Swords Hist Soc. see page 152.

Westpalstown, Oldtown:
MEMS: Dublin Vol. 5; Also indexed by Swords Hist Soc. see p.152.

Whitechurch (Moravian):
Memorial Inscriptions of Ireland Vol 1. - GSI; also at www.academia.edu/9320608

Whitechurch (New), Rathfarnham:
MEMS: Dublin Vol. 4.

Whitechurch (Old), Rathfarnham:
MEMS: Dublin Vol. 3; & Ir. Gen. 8(1) 1990, pp. 111-121.

Whitestown (Rush):
MEMS: Dublin Vol. 8, also indexed by Swords Hist Soc. see p.152.

Civilian Burials
in Carrickbrennan Graveyard

Name	Year	No.	Name	Year	No.
Abbot Frances	1852	231	Ball Anna	1906	112
Abbot John Jnr	1865	231	Ball E.G.	1850	112
Abbot John Snr	1856	231	Ball Florinda	1873	112
Abbot Joseph	1866	291	Barry Fran	1770	143
Abbot Mary	1846	231	Bateman Charles W.M.	1849	408
Adam William	1816	081	Bateman Isabella	1809	408
Allan Helena Maria	1857	109	Battersby Henry John	1868	408
Allt Rebecca	1840	433	Battersby Sarah		249
Anderson Alexander	1818	362	Baxter John	1874	164
Andrews George	1843	175	Baxter Kate	1888	164
Andrews Honor	1841	175	Baxter Richard	1871	164

	Lord Mayors.	Sheriffs.
1735	Sir Richard Grattan, 9 months. / George Forbes, 3 ditto.	Robert King, John Twigg
1736	James Somervell	Richard White, Edward Hunt
1737	William Walker	Charles Rossell, Robert Ross
1738	John Macarrell	Thomas Baker, George Ripton
1739	Daniel Falkiner	J. Bern. Hoffshleger, John Adamson
1740	Sir Samuel Cook	James Dunn, Benjamin Hunt
1741	William Aldrich	W. Grattan, Q. Somervell, T. Read
1742	Gilbert King	George Fraser, John Bradshaw
1743	David Tew / William Aldrich	George Swettenham, Thomas Broughton
1744	John Walker	Daniel Walker, Patrick Ewing
1745	Daniel Cooke	John Espinase, Andrew Murray
1746	Richard White / William Walker	William Cooke, Thomas Taylor
1747	Sir George Ripton	John Hornby, John Cooke
1748	Robert Ross	Matthew Weld, Hans Bailie
1749	John Adamson / Sir Samuel Cooke	Thomas Mead, Robert Donovan
1750	Thomas Taylor	George Reynolds, Thomas White
1751	John Cooke	James Taylor, John Tew
1752	Sir Charles Burton	John Forbes, Patrick Hamilton
1753	Andrew Murray	Edmond Huband, H. Wray, Alexander Ry
1754	Hans Bailie	Philip Crampton, Timothy Allen
1755	Percival Hunt	Arthur Lamprey, Charles Rossell
1756	John Forbes	Peter Barré, Charles Nobileau
1757	Thomas Mead	Michael Sweeney, William Forbes
1758	Philip Crampton	Benjamin Geale, James Taylor
1759	John Tew	Benjamin Barton, Edward Sankey
1760	Sir Patrick Hamilton	Francis Fetherston, George Wrightson
1761	Sir Timothy Allen	Mathew Bailie, Thomas Blackall
1762	Charles Rossell	John Read, Joseph Hall
1763	William Forbes	William Brien, Francis Booker
1764	Benjamin Geale	Henry Hart, Robert Montgomery
1765	James Taylor	William Rutledge, Richard French
1766	Edward Sankey	William Lightburne, Thomas Emerson
1767	Francis Featherstone	P. Boyde, H. Bevan
1768	Benjamin Barton	William Dunn, Henry Williams
1769	Sir T. Blackhall	Kilner Sweetman, An. King
1770	George Reynolds	Blen. Grove, Ant. Porrier
1771	F. Booker / W. Forbes	James Hamilton, James Horan
1772	Richard French	James Shiels, James Jones
1773	Willoughby Lightburne	Nat. Warren, John Tucker
1774	Henry Hart	John Wilson, Thomas Truelock
1775	T. Emerson	Fielding Ould, Geo. Alcock, Thomas Be
1776	Henry Bevan	John Rose, William Alexander
1777	William Dunn	Henry Howison, Henry Gore Sankey
1778	S. A. King	William Worthington, Richard Moncrie
1779	James Hamilton	William James, John Exshaw
1780	Kil. Sweetenham	P. Bride, Thomas Andrews
1781	John Darragh	James Campbell, David Dick
1782	Nathaniel Warren	John Carlton, Samuel Read
1783	Thomas Green	Alexander Kirkpatrick, Benjamin Smith
1784	James Horan	Caleb Jenkin, Ambrose Leet
1785	James Shiel	John Sankey, Hugh Trevor
1786	George Alcock	William Thompson, Thomas Fleming
1787	William Alexander	William Humfrey, Brent. Nevill
1788	William Rose	Thomas Tweedy, Jeremiah D'Olier
1789	John Exshaw	Charles Thorpe, James Vance
1790	Henry Howison	Joseph Dickinson, James Williams
1791	Henry Gore Sankey	Benjamin Gault, John Norton

18th century Mayors and Sheriffs of Dublin
from Warburton's 'History of the city of Dublin from the earliest accounts to the present time'.... (1818)

Chapter 9   Newspapers

The earliest known Irish newspaper was published in 1649, and during the 18th century the numbers greatly increased so that by the 1900 Dublin had seen the publication of 70 different newspaper titles.

The family history information in newspapers includes birth, marriage and death notices, business notices, petitions and court proceedings. However, these notices usually refer to wealthier families. Newspapers can, however, provide excellent details of people involved in many other activities.

Surviving newspapers for Dublin are at the NLI, DCLA, and the British Library (BL). Some of these collections are incomplete.

Many Irish newspapers are now available online. The pay-per-view site, Irish Newspaper Archives (www.irishnewsarchive.com), offers access to many national (e.g. The Nation and the Freeman's Journal) and local papers. The pay site www.findmypast.ie has an extensive collection and the Irish Times (www.irishtimes.com) has digitized all its issues from 1859 to date.

Arguably the best Dublin newspapers for the eighteenth century are Faulkner's Dublin Journal, the Freeman's Journal, Dublin Hibernian Journal, and the Dublin Evening Post. Nineteenth century publications include the Dublin Morning Post, Dublin Evening Herald, and Dublin Evening Mail. A card index to biographical notices in Faulkner's Dublin Journal from 1763-71 is held in the National Library of Ireland.

Other useful indexes are:
Marriages in Dublin Newspapers 1731-1740. GO Ms. 665.
Marriage announcements from Exshaw's Magazine (1741-1800) and *Hibernian Magazine (1771-1800)* (Chronologically listed) GO Ms. 131-133.
Notices of Marriages and Deaths from London Magazine 1747-49. NLI Ms. 4492.
Press Cuttings of Births, Marriages and Deaths 1848-72 & 1873-1904. (with name index) GO Ms 445-446 (Ryan Collection)

An Index to marriages in *Walker's Hibernian Magazine 1771-1812)* compiled by Henry Farrar has been published as 'Irish Marriages' (London 1897).

Listed below are the main newspapers for the city and county; and the holdings of each in the National Library (NLI) and the British Library (BL) or elsewhere where relevant. Note that there are many other newspapers in both archives, and full indexes to their collections are available. Note also that many newspapers changed their title due to new management, mergers etc. These changes are also indicated. Also shown is the start and end date (month/year) of the holdings of each archive. Where indexes or published abstracts are available, this is also indicated.

Constitution and Church Sentinel
Published in: Dublin, 1849-53
BL Holdings: 4.1849-5.1853

Correspondent
Published in: Dublin, 1806-61
Note: continued as Dublin Correspondent in 1822; Evening Packet and Correspondent in 1828; Evening Packet in 1860
NLI Holdings: 11.1806-12.1861
BL Holdings: 11.1806-4.1810; odd numbers 1810-11, 1813-16, 1820; 1-12.1823; odd numbers 1825, 26

Dublin Chronicle
Published in: Dublin, 1762-1817 Note: breaks in publication
NLI Holdings: 1.1770-12.1771; 5.1787-12.1793; odd numbers 6.1815-1817
BL Holdings: 5.1787-4.1792; 5-12.1793

Dublin Courant
Published in: Dublin, 1702-25; New Series: 1744-50
NLI Holdings: odd numbers 1703, 1705; 6.1744-2.1752; many issues missing
BL Holdings: odd numbers 1718-20, 22, 1.1723-12.1725; 4.1744-3.1750

Dublin Evening Mail (contd. as Evening Mail)
Published in: Dublin, 1823-1962
NLI Holdings: 2.1823-7.1962
Gilbert Lib. Holdings: 1845; 1860-64; 1900-1940
BL Holdings: 2.1823-2.1928

Dublin Evening Post
Published in: Dublin, 1732-37 and 1778-1875
NLI Holdings: 6.1732-1.1737; 2.1778-8.1875
Gilbert Lib. Holdings: 1812-43 (odd issues); 1825-27; 1830-32; 1834-41;1843-51
BL Holdings: 6.1732-7.1734; 7.1737-7.1741; 8.1778-7.1753; 10.1783-12.1785; 1787; 1789; 1792; 1794; 5-6.1795;1.1796-12.1797; 1.1804-12.1810; odd numbers 1813, 14; 1.1815-8.1875

Dublin Gazette (contd. as Iris Oifigiul in 1922)
Published in: Dublin, 1705-current
Note: Mainly Government notices
NLI Holdings: 11.1706-12.1727; 3.1729-4.1744; 6.1756-12.1759; 1760; 1762; 1763; 1765; 1766; 1767; 1-7.1775; 1776-88; 1790-1921; Index to Marriages and Deaths (1730-1740) in NLI Ms. 3197

Dublin Gazette and Weekly Courant
Published in: Dublin, 1703-28
NLI Holdings: odd numbers 1708

Dublin Intelligence
Published in: Dublin, 1690-1725 (at various times)
NLI Holdings: 9.1690-5.1693
BL Holdings: odd numbers 1708-12, 1723-25

Dublin Journal - see Faulkner's Dublin Journal.

Dublin Mercury (contd. as Hoey's Dublin Mercury in 1770)
Published in: Dublin, 1704-75
NLI Holdings: 12.1722-5.1724; 1-9.1726; 1-9.1742; 3-9.1770; 9.1770-4.1773
BL Holdings: 1-9.1742; 3.1766-4.1773

Dublin Morning Post (contd. as Carricks Morning Post in 1804-21)
Published in: Dublin, c. 1804-32
NLI Holdings: 4.1814-1831
BL Holdings: odd numbers 1824-26; 1.1830-5.1832

Evening Freeman
Published in: Dublin, 1831-71
NLI Holdings: 8.1831-7.1836; 4-12.1844; 1845-9.1847; odd numbers
1848; 2.1858-59
BL Holdings: 1.1831-6.1871

Evening Herald
Published in: Dublin, 1786-1814; new series 1891-in progress
NLI Holdings: 5.1786-12.1789; 1.1806-12.1809; odd numbers 1810;
1.1812-6.1814
BL Holdings: 5.1786-12.1789; odd numbers 1807, 1813; 12.1891-in
progress. See p.110.

Evening Irish Times
Published in: Dublin, c. 1860-1921
NLI Holdings: 4.1896-3.1900; 7.1900-3.1901; 7.1901-1907; 1911-
6.1915
BL Holdings: 10.1880-10.1921

Evening Packet (later incorporated with Dublin Evening Mail)
Published in: Dublin, 1828-62
BL Holdings: 1.1828-4.1929; 9.1829-3.1862

Evening Telegraph
Published in: Dublin, 1871-1924
NLI Holdings: 10.1884-12.1924
Gilbert Lib. Holdings: incomplete 1897-1924
BL Holdings: 7.1871-11.1873; 8.1875-5.1916; 1.1919-12.1924

Faulkner's Dublin Journal
Published in: Dublin, 1725-1825
NLI Holdings: 1.1726-7.1735; 5.1736-1782; 1787-90; 1.1791-4.1825
BL Holdings: odd numbers 1726, 1739-40; 3.1741; 8-12.1744; 3.1748-
3.1750; 3.1751-12.1764; 12.1765-12.1768; odd numbers 1782-84, 1792;
1-12.1796; odd numbers 1798, 99, 1803; 10.1804-12.1810; odd numbers
1813-14, 1817; 12.1819-12.1821

THE IRISH GENEALOGIST

his only Son the Hon Garret Wesley, Representative for the Borough of Trim. Mr John Vaughan formerly a Grocer in New Church-street. Yesterday Mrs Parker Wife of Admiral Parker.

3209. Sat. 4–Tues. 7 Feb.
Marriages. Last Week Mr Stephen Nix of Kileage County Kildare, to Miss Elinor Vincent of Killybeggs in said Co Last Saturday Mark Tew of Raddinstown Co Meath, Esq, to Miss Leland, with £3,000 Fortune. Mr Richard Magee of Fownes-street to Miss Susanna Hyde of Capel-street, with a handsome Fortune.
Deaths. Last Tuesday at Corke, Mr Edward Stockdall and Mr Richard Moore, both eminent Chandlers. Last Week Mr William Sinclair, Merchant.

3210. Tues. 7–Sat. 11 Feb.
Marriages. Last Week James Collins, of Rathcoole Esq, to Miss Diana Coakley Daughter of Abraham Coakley Esq, near Kanturk. Mr Richard Burke of Derrimacloghny, Co Galway, to Miss Catherine Burke.
Deaths. On 27 of last month at Bath, the Hon Miss Molesworth. Last Sunday in the County of Wexford the Rev Archdeacon Curtis. At Naas in an advanced Age, Mrs Graydon, a Widow Gentlewoman. Wednesday Mrs Percival Wife of William Percival Esq, of Ballyhamon, Co Wexford. In Anglesea-street Mrs Oliver.

3211. Sat. 11–Tues. 14 Feb.
Marriages. A few Days ago at Ballyshannon, Henry Major of Camlin Esq, to Miss Sally Scanlan, with a handsome Fortune. Last Week Mr Thomas Richardson of Durrow, to Miss Ann Phillips of Foyle.
Deaths. Last Tuesday in Caple-street Mr Nicholas Hadsor, in a very advanced Age. He was the eldest Surgeon in this City. Sunday in Aungier-street Capt John Arabine of Col Campbell's Regiment of Dragoons and only Son of Colonel Arabine who lately died at Gibraltar. In Essex-street Mr Taylor, Merchant.

3212. Tues. 14–Sat. 18 Feb.
Marriage. Last Week, Mr William Morton of Tinihely, Co Wicklow, to Miss Martha Wood-worth, of Earl-street, with a large Fortune.
Deaths. Lately, Charles McDermot of Shufe, of Coolavin, Co Sligo, Esq, commonly called Prince of Coolavin, aged 98, a gentleman of the old Faith who to the very Last retained all the antient grandeur of the old Faith. Last Tuesday Mrs Hamilton, Wife of Alexander Hamilton, Esq, and Representative in Parliament for Killeagh. Thursday morning in Fleet-street aged 95 Lieut Charles St Ferrol, who served H M King William in his Wars and again at the Breach of the Boyne. In Fleet-street Mr Martin Carthy Cook to Trinity College. In Dame-street, the Wife of Mr Fitzsimons, Baker. At Priesthouse near this City, Mr William Callaghan, Farmer. In Aungier-street, Counsellor Frederick Trench.

3213. Sat. 18–Tues. 21 Feb.
Death. Last Saturday, Mrs Huddleston, Wife of Mr Chapman Huddleston Attorney, who by her death will be entitled to £1,500.

3214. Tues. 21–Sat. 25 Feb.
Marriage. A few Days ago, Mr Logan, Staymaker of Lazer's Hill, to Miss Crow of Fleet-street with a handsome Fortune.
Deaths. Last Week at Douneen Co Corke, the Wife of Mr Dennis M'Carthy. On Kerl's Quay Corke, in an advanced Age, Mr John Kesterson. Sunday in Fleet-street, Mrs Elizabeth Finlay of Fleet-street. Monday at Stephen's Green, an advanced Age, Mrs Oliver, Relict of the late Colonel Oliver mother of Philip Oliver one of the representatives in Parliament for the Borough

Biographical notices are often published in family history journals,
the above example is from
'Faulkner's Dublin Journal' 1758 – in the Irish Genealogist 11(2) (2003)
see: http://www.irishancestors.ie/

COAL FUND FOR DUBLIN,

MEETING IN THE MANSION HOUSE,

Yesterday, at four o'clock, a meeting was held in the Oak Room of the Mansion House by invitation of the Right Hon the Lord Mayor, for the purpose of establishing a Coal Fund for Dublin. The heads of the charitable organisations of Dublin and all interested in the establishment of a fund of the kind were specially invited; and amongst those present were—

R W Smyth, Hon Secretary Society for Relief of Distressed Protestants; Rev P B Johnson, Dublin Superintendent Irish Church Missions; George D Williams, 45 Molesworth street; John Irwin, 121 Upper Abbey street; Edward Kevans, 22 Dame street; Rev W B Lumley, 15 Harrington street; Rev Harvey Stewart, Dublin Parochial Association; J Haveron, C E, 28 York street, Dublin; Rev Robert Staples, C C, Francis street;

An extract from the Freeman's Journal 14th December 1897

Freeman's Journal or Public Register
Published in: Dublin, 1763-1924
Gilbert Lib. Holdings: 1763-1924 (mf.)
BL Holdings: odd numbers 1784; odd numbers 1823-1833; 1.1837-12.1924

General Advertiser
Published in: Dublin, 1804-1924
NLI Holdings: 9.1804-11.1820; odd numbers 1837; 2.1841-12.1851; 1853-54, 1857-61; 1864; 1866-67; 1869-70; 1874-12.1877; 1.1880-1890; 1892-3.1924
BL Holdings: 10.1838-12.1840 (with gaps); odd numbers 1841, 1846; 12.1846-7.1914; 1.1915-12.1923

Impartial Occurrences (contd. as Pue's Occurrences in 1714)
Published in: Dublin, 1704-80
NLI Holdings: 12.1704-2.1706; 12.1718-1748; 1751-1755; 1.1756-5.1757; 4-12.1768
BL Holdings: 1.1705-2.1706; odd numbers 1714, 1719, 1740; 1.1741-12.1742; 1.1744-12.1749; 1.1752-12.1753; 1.1756-12.1758; 1761
Index to Marriages and Deaths (1730-1740 in NLI Ms. 3197)

Irish Times
Published in: Dublin, 1859-current
Gilbert Lib. Holdings: 1859-1950 (mf.)
NLI Holdings: 3.1859-in progress
BL Holdings: 3.1859-in progress (except part of 11.1871).
The Irish Times digital archive is on-line at www.irishtimes.com.
see also Evening Irish Times and Weekly Irish Times.

Kingstown Gazette
Published in: Kingstown/Dun Laoghaire, old series 1857-58; new series 1868-69
Gilbert Lib. Holdings: 12.1857-1.1858, 5.1868-7.1869 (mf.)
BL Holdings: 12.1857-1.1858; 5.1868-7.1869

Magee's Weekly Packet
Published in: Dublin, 1777-93
NLI Holdings: 6.1777-3.1895; 3.1787-8.1790; 8.1792-8.1793
BL Holdings: 6-10.1777; 11.1777-3.1785; odd numbers to 1793

Morning Mail
Published in: Dublin, 1870-1912
NLI Holdings: 2.1870-12.1883
Gilbert Lib. Holdings: 1878; 1880
BL Holdings: 3.1871-6.1880; 12.1896-8.1912 (with gaps)

Morning Register
Published in: Dublin, 1824-43
NLI Holdings: 10.1824-1.1843
Gilbert Lib. Holdings: 1835-36; 1840; 1842.
BL Holdings: 10.1824-1.1843

FETE CHAMPETRE,

For the Benefit of the Mendicity Institution,

ON SATURDAY, June the 8th, under the Patronage of his Excellency the LORD LIEUTENANT, who has kindly consented to be present. To take place at the Lodge of Lord Morpeth, in the Phœnix Park.

COMMITTEE OF MANAGEMENT:

The Right Hon. the Lord Mayor.
The High Sheriffs, Grant and Taylor.

Captain Wynyard	Captain Somerset
Captain Williams, A.D.C.	James S. Molloy, Esq.
Captain G. Hume	Cornelius Lyne, Esq.
Acheson Lyle, Esq.	Lieutenant-Colonel Cobbe, Royal Artillery,
Richard Bourke, Esq.	
Corry Connellan, Esq.	Major White, 6th Dragoons
Wm. Dean Freeman, Esq.	Major St. Quinton, 17th Lancers
George French, Esq., Q.C.	
Major White	Lieut.-Colonel Hamilton, 19th Regiment
St. John Blacker, Esq.	
Sir E. Borough, Bart.	Colonel Falconer, 22d Regt.
Charles Fox, Esq.	Major Cockburne, 60th Rifles
William Kemmis, Esq.	Major Halifax, 75th Regt.
William Brownlow, Esq.	Major Eden, 88th Regiment.
Richard Cane, Esq.	Colonel Webber Smith
Edward Cane, Esq.	Colonel Holloway
Richard Armit, Esq.	Lieutenant-Colonel King
Fredk. Willis, Esq., A.D.C.	Lieut.-Colonel Campbell, 97th Regiment
J. R. Corballis, Esq.	
Hon. J. Fortescue, A.D.C.	Captain Trevor.
Hon. R. Bruce	W. N. Barry, Esq., 8th Hussars,
Hon. D. Plunket,	
Colonel D'Aguilar,	John Hamilton, Esq.
Thomas Forde, Esq.	Thomas Wilson, Esq.
Captain King, R N.	Alderman West,
Bolton Massey, Esq.	Sison Cooper, Esq.
Charles T. Webber, Esq.	Robert Burrowes, Esq.,
J. Smily, Esq.	Philip Doyne, Esq.
Sir William Leeson,	Sir Thomas Staples, Bart.
Wyndham Goold, Esq.	Major Hodgson, 19th Regt.

Tickets to be had of the Members of the Committee, or at the Committee Room, Commercial Buildings, between the hours of Two and Five o'Clock, from Monday, 3d June, to Thursday, the 6th of June.

Admission from the Fifteen Acres, at Two o'Clock. *Dejune* at Four precisely.

Ladies' Ticket,	...	...	10s. 0d.
Gentlemen's Ticket,	...		12s. 6d.

(Tickets not transferable.)

THOMAS WRIGHT, } Secretaries to the Com-
HENRY HALIDAY, Esqrs. } mittee of Management.

An extract from Saunder's Newsletter ~ 3rd June 1839
- see page 119

Nation (contd. as Daily Nation and Weekly Nation)
Published in: Dublin, 1842-1900
NLI Holdings: 10.1842-7.1891; 6.1896-9.1900
Gilbert Lib. Holdings: 1842-73; 1873-76; 1880-1884
BL Holdings: 10.1824-7.1848; 9.1849-7.1891; 6.1896-9.1900

Patriot (contd. as Statesman and Patriot in 1828)
Published in: Dublin, c.1810-29
NLI Holdings: 7.1810-1815; 1818-10.1828; 11.1829-5.1829
BL Holdings: 1.1823-10.1828

Pue's Occurrences - see Impartial Occurrences

Saunder's Newsletter (contd. as Saunder's Irish Daily News in 1878)
Published in: Dublin, 1755-1879
NLI Holdings: odd numbers 1767-91; 3.1773-12.1787; 1.1789-3.1795;
2.1796-12.1802; 4.1804-12.1806; 1.1808-11.1809; 1812-18; 1820-
11.1879
Gilbert Lib. Holdings: 1858; 1861
BL Holdings: 3.1773-12.1787; 1789; 1.1793-12.1794; 1795; 1.1797-
12.1811; 1.1813-12.1815; 1.1817-11.1879 See p.118

The Warder (continued as Sports Mail and Irish Weekly Mail in 1921)
Published in: Dublin, 1821-1939
NLI Holdings: 3.1821-9.1938
BL Holdings: 3.1822-9.1939 (except 1930)

Weekly Freeman's Journal (continued as Weekly Freeman, National
Press and Irish Agriculturist in 1892)
Published in: Dublin, c.1817-1924
NLI Holdings: 1-7.1818; 3-7.1830; 1.1834-4.1840; 6.1880-12.1882;
5.1883-3.1892; 4.1892-12.1893; 1.1895-12.1913; 6.1914-12.1924
BL Holdings: 10.1821-12.1831; 1.1838-3.1892; 4.1892-12.1924

Weekly Irish Times (contd. as Times Pictorial in 1941)
Published in: Dublin, 1875-1941
NLI Holdings: odd numbers 1875; 1.1883-6.1886; 1.1906-11.1941
BL Holdings: 6.1875-12.1920; 1.1922-11.1941

Diocese of Dublin   Parish of Balrothery

TOWNLAND.	NAMES OF OCCUPIERS.	Quantities in Detail.			Quality.	Total Quantity in Holding.			Total Quantity in Townland.			Real Acreable Value.		
Castleland	John Wade	19	3	14	4	19	3	14	19	3	14	1	16	-
	James Wade	19	2	30	4	19	2	30	19	2	30	1	16	-
	Jane Dalton widow	1	3	19	4	1	2	19	1	2	19	1	10	-
	John Berry	5	2	18	4	5	2	18	5	2	18	1	16	-
	No. John Smith	4	-	23	4	4	-	23	4	3	23	1	16	-
	Thomas Rooney	4	3	17	4	4	3	17	4	3	17	1	16	-
	Thomas Boyle	3	1	9	4	3	1	9	3	1	9	1	16	-
	Thomas Dennis	5		9	4	5		9	5		9	1	16	-

An extract from the Tithe Applotment Books for the townland of Castleland in the civil parish of Balrothery.

Chapter 10   Land Records

In a primarily agricultural country, ownership or use of land was highly important. In addition, it was a major political issue as dispossession of land, and on occasion its planting with settlers, had widely occurred. Various land records therefore exist. To understand these records, it is useful to know that land could be owned outright, leased on a long-term basis (for a period of years or for the duration of the lives of specified persons), or rented on a short-term basis (very often at the whim of the landlord or his agent). During the 18th and early 19th century, the occupiers of the land were generally not its owners. They were small farmers and cottiers who rented or leased the land from large estates. The major land records and their significance is described below

Record/Source	Period	What is recorded
Registry of Deeds	1708 -	Sales, mortgages, leases etc.
Tithe Applotment Survey	1821-1846	Landholdings (arable)
Griffith Valuation Survey	1848-52	Building and land holdings
Encumbered Estates Court	mid 1800's -	Insolvent estate owners and tenants
Estate Records	All periods	Names of tenants, agents and workers
Land Registry	1897 -	Owners of land

Tithe Applotment Survey

Tithes were taxes levied on arable land for the upkeep of the CoI. Prior to 1832 they were paid 'in kind' in the form of farm produce etc. From that year a Commissioner was appointed for each parish to oversee valuation of properties and 'applotment' of tithes based on that valuation. The Tithe Applotment (or Composition) Books produced show: townland, name of occupier, area and tithe payable. They are available on line at http://titheapplotmentbooks.nationalarchives.ie/search/tab/home.jsp In urban areas a similar levy called 'Minister's Money' was applied, but few records survive.

Griffith's Primary Valuation

Griffith's Primary Valuation was carried out in Dublin between 1848 and 1852. Its purpose was to calculate a relative 'valuation' of each holding. A tax, commonly called 'rates', was levied based on this valuation. The resulting records show, for each property or landholding, the following: Parish and Townland or Street; Map reference; Name of occupier; Description of the holding (or 'tenement'); Area; Rateable value of property. An index compiled by the NLI is available in many archives and free on-line at http://www.askaboutireland.ie/griffith-valuation/ It is also available on FMP. It is particularly useful for locating a person within the county. For the city it is less useful as only the householder is named, whereas many properties in poorer areas were occupied by many families.

Further valuations of properties were conducted up to modern times. These can be inspected in "Cancellation Books" at the Valuation Office in Dublin. Copies of the primary valuations are in the NAI, National Library, Gilbert Library and most of the larger libraries.

Registry of Deeds.

A deed is a written witnessed agreement or undertaking by one or more parties. The vast majority deal with property transactions, e.g. leases, mortgages and conveyances. Business partnerships and marriage settlements were also registered. The Registry of Deeds was established in 1708 as a repository where deeds could be officially registered, but registration was not compulsory (see www.landregistry.ie). The complete set of registered deeds is in the Registry of Deeds, Henrietta Street, Dublin. There are two sets of indexes which can be used to locate a deed, a Grantors Index and a Land Index.

Grantors Index: These are volumes arranged by initial letter of surname and a time-frame. e.g. A 1708-1729. The Grantor Index Books for the years 1708-1832 are arranged as follows: Surname and forename of grantor; surname (only) of grantee; volume, page and number of the transcript. From 1833, the arrangement is: Surname and forename of grantor; surname and forename of grantee; Location of land (not always stated); year of registration; and transcript volume and number. See Registry of Deeds Index Project Ireland at http://irishdeedsindex.net/index.html

Land Index: As there is no grantee index, and the name of the grantor is not known the land index may be used. These are arranged by time frame for each county. Some deeds were registered giving no indication of barony, so the 'no barony' books for the relative time-frame should be checked also.

Transcript Books: These contain verbatim transcripts of the original deeds. They are highly complex documents, hand-written and often difficult to read although the biographical information can usually be extracted without understanding the legal jargon.

Memorial: A memorial is the copy of the deed registered by the parties. It is from this deed that the transcription is made. Photocopies of these can be obtained. A volunteer project has indexed about 24,000 memorials and has generated almost 225,000 records. The index is at: http://irishdeedsindex.net/

Abstract Books: These give details about the parties involved in agreements and transactions. There are no abstracts for 1708-1832.

Pre 1708 Deeds: A collection of pre-1708 deeds for Dublin (approx 200 for the city and 100 for the county) are held at the NAI where a card-index can be consulted. The cards are arranged by barony and note place, date, parties to deed, nature of deed and ref. no.

Encumbered Estates

Under the Encumbered Estates Act of 1849 the Encumbered Estates Court (later the Landed Estates Court) was established and empowered to sell, auction or transfer the estates of insolvent or 'encumbered' owners. They can also be searched on the pay-for site www.findmypast.ie.

Documents for the estates auctioned are held in the NAI and NLI. The O'Brien Rental Index, the Encumbered Estates Court Index to Conveyances, the Landed Estates Court Records of Conveyances and the Landed Estates Court Index can be consulted to obtain references for these records.

The Land Registry

In 1892 the Land registry was established to provide a system of compulsory registration of title of land bought under various land purchase acts. When title is registered all the relevant details are entered into numbered folios. The details in each folio are divided under the following headings: (i) Property location and barony (ii) Ownership (iii) Burdens.

Maps relating to all registrations are also held by the Land Registry. A folio can be located by a name index search (when the registered owner is known) or a map search (when the address is known). All title registrations for Dublin are held by the Land Registry, Chancery Street, Dublin 7 and can be accessed by personal callers.

Estate Records

The classic land ownership in Ireland until the 1880s was the Estate, i.e. a very large holding of land which was rented in large or small sections to tenants. This included city properties. The rental activity, leasing, tenant evictions and the other maintenance of these estates produced records. Such estate records can sometimes provide information about an ancestor who rented land from, or worked on, an estate. However, estate records are private and there is no central repository for those which are now on public access. They are in various national and local archives while many still remain in private hands.

Estate records generally consist of any or all of the following: rentals, maps, deeds, wage books or letters. To locate estate records, it is necessary to know the owner of the estate. This can be established by consulting one of the following:

(i) The 'lessor' column of the Griffith's Valuations, although in many cases the lessor named is subletting from the estate owner.
(ii) The Land Owners of Ireland by U.H. Hussey deBurgh (1878).
(iii) OS Fieldname books.

The following table shows a small selection of Dublin estate records held in the main repositories. It is arranged by family or estate name, a brief description of the contents, a time frame and the reference.

Family/Estate	Description /	Timeframe	Reference
Allingham	see Carroll		
Ambrose	see Eccles		
Apjohn	Documents relating to properties	1826-1906	NAI M.5377
Archer	see Carroll		
Ashburn	90 deeds	1325-60	TCD Ms.1027
Atkins	see Apjohn		
Ball	see Mullen		
Bateman	see Greene		
Bell	see Mullen		
Biggs	see Cassidy		
Brabazon	see Hayes		
Brandy	see Hayes		
Bryan	see Rawlins		
Bulfin	see Thomson		
Bury	see Smyth		
Busby	see Horton		
Byrne	see Clancy		
Caddell	see Newcomen		
Cadell	see Gordon		
Caldwell	Wills and deeds	1779-1828	NAI T.10,869, 16,952-5
Callwell	see Caldwell		
Carew	see Greene		
Carroll	Deeds	1608-1871	NAI D.16,971-99
Cassidy	80 deeds relating to property with some Wills	Late 19th/ early 20th centuries	NLI D.7956-8035
Cavendish	see Carroll		
Christ Church	List of leases	1577-1644	NAI M.2534
Clancy	75 deeds relating to properties and some Wills	19th century	NAI D.7708-7782
Clarke	see Coates		
Clements	see Newcomen		

Family/Estate	Description	Timeframe	Reference
Coard	see Mullen and Ball		
Coates	41 deeds relating to properties and some Wills	19th century	NAI D.7915-7955
Collins	see O'Connor		
Connor	see Smyth		
Cooke	see Greene		
Coskey	see Pennefather		
Croker	see Greene		
Cusack	18 deeds	19th Century	NLI D.10,851 - 68
Daly	see Finnegan		
Darley	Rent ledger. see also Smyth	1822-1852	NLI Ms.5806
Dawson	see Gordon		
Delahunt	see Larne		
Delany	see Gordon (1703-1897)		
Despard	see Rawlins		
Digby	see Newcomen		
Dixon	see Horton		
Domville	Rentals with some accounts	1750-1753	NLI Ms.11,818
Domville	List of leases	1760-1850	NLI Ms.11,790
Domville	Rentals	1839-1845	NLI Ms.11,817
Domville	Misc. Documents	19th century	NLI Ms.11,792
Donlon	see O'Connor		
Dowdall	see Smyth		
Eager	see Newcomen		
Eccles	Documents relating to property	n.d.	
Ellis	see White		
Ellis	see Hackett		
Essebourne	see Ashburn		
Farrell	see Hackett		
Fay	see Thomson		

Family/Estate	Description /	Timeframe	Reference
Fingall (Earl)	Rent Roll	1738-1982	NLI Ms.4898
Finnegan	70 deeds relating to property with some Wills	Late 19th/ early 20th centuries	NLI D.7541-7610
Fitzgerald	see O'Connor		
Fitzwilliam	Rentals and disbursements	1754-69	NLI P.943
Flanagan	see Cassidy		
Flood	see Clancy		
Foot	14 deeds	c.1806-1820	NLI D.9511 - 9524
Freeman	see Mullen		
Gleadowe	see Gordon		
Goodwin	see Smyth		
Gordon	73 deeds	Late 18th/ early 19th centuries	NAI D.7468-7490
Gordon	Papers relating to properties	1703-1897	NAI D.17,178-282, M.2066-68, T.7101-10
Greene	Papers relating to property	1790-1877	NAI D.17,283-302, T.7112-14
Guinness	see Toomey		
Hackett	75 deeds relating to properties and some Wills	19th century	NAI D.8345-8419
Ham	Papers relating to estate	Early 19th century	NAI Hoey and Donning parcel 26.
Hamilton	Papers relating to property	19th century	NAI M.5571
Hardy	see Newcomen		
Harris	see Mullen		
Hatch	Deeds, bonds, Wills and marriage settlements	Late 17th - 19th century	NLI D.19.439-658

Family/Estate	Description	Timeframe	Reference
Hayes	66 deeds relating to properties	19th century	NLI D.8609-8684
Hearn	see Hackett		
Heatley	see Eccles		
Higginbotham	see Carroll		
Higginson	see Rawlins		
Hobart	see Rawlins		
Hopkins	see Cassidy		
Hopkins	Rent rolls	1795-96, 1800, 1839	
Horton	132 deeds and some Wills	18th century	NLI D.7783-7827, 7828-7875, 7876-7914
Howe	see White		
Hughes	see Horton		
Johnson	Papers relating to house property	1782-1853	NAI Hoey and Donning parcel 29.
Kearney	see Coates		
Kelly	see Finnegan		
Lane	7 deeds (Photostats)	1687-1704	NLI D.11,433-9
Langley	see Hackett		
Larne	Papers relating to property	1753-1841	NAI D.17,404-18, T.7126
Leech	see Clancy		
Lindop	see Gordon (1703-1897)		
Lloyd	see Apjohn		
Locke	Property	1703-1810	NAI D.20,273-93, M.3334-9
Lord	see Carroll		
Lynch	see Horton		
Madden	see Horton		
Maguiness	see Clancy		
Maher	see Hackett		
Maher	see Coates		
Martin	see Hackett		
McAllester	see Carroll		
McCallery	see Horton		

Family/Estate	Description	Timeframe	Reference
McConchy	Deeds and press cuttings relating to the C of I	Late 17th to 20th century	Unsorted collection in NLI
McDonnell	see Thomson		
McGennis	see Toomey		
McNamara	see Hackett		
Meagher	see Horton		
Middleton	see Horton		
Molloy	see Horton		
Moore	34 deeds relating to property	1527-1764	NLI D.21,596 - 21,629
Morgell	see Larne		
Mullen	88 deeds relating to property	Late 19th/ early 20th centuries	NAI D.8257-8344
Mullet	see White		
Murphy	see Clancy		
Murphy	see Cassidy		
Nagle	see Gordon (1703-1897)		
Newcomen	42 deeds relating to property	Late 18th/ 19th century	NLI D.7426-67
Nolan	see Finnegan		
O'Connor	65 deeds	Late 19th century	NAI D.8493-8557
O'Farrell	see Thomson		
Oldham	see Larne		
Palmerston	see Temple		
Parke	see Horton		
Pembroke	see Fitzwilliam		
Pembroke Estate	Printed calendar of deeds	1225-1727	NAI D.19,299
Pennefather	Papers relating to property	1745-1898	NAI D.17,597-736, M.2090-2175
Plunkett	Fingal papers	1509-1838	NLI Ms.
Preston	Transcripts of documents	covering the 12th -15th century	NLI Ms.1646

Family/Estate	Description	Timeframe	Reference
Rainsford	Papers relating to property	1829-91	NAI M.5751 (1-8)
Rawlins	Papers relating to property	1757-1915	NAI M.
Reynolds	see Coates		
Rooney	see White		
Ross	see Eccles		
Ryan	see Horton		
Ryan	see Hackett		
Ryder	see Carroll		
Ryves	see Pennefather		
Saunders	see Pennefather		
Scott	see Hackett		
Shaw	Leases and financial documents	c.1707-1850	NLI Ms.8939
Sheil	see Cassidy		
Smith	see Hayes		
Smyth	House property	1703-1898	NAI D.17,966-18,037, T.7194-5
St. Anne (Guild)	12 boxes of documents	14th-19th century	RIA Mss. 12 8, 22-33
Stamer	see Rawlins		
Staples	see White		
Stewart	Rentals	1797-1807	NLI Ms.5944-45
Temple	Rentals	1788-1796	NLI Ms.1566
Terry	see Toomey		
Thomson	87 deeds relating to properties	1854-1904	NLI D.8098-8185
Toomey	73 deeds relating to property with some Wills	Late 19th century	NLI D.8420-8492
Towers	see Thomson		
Tucker	see Horton		
Tucker	see Hayes		
Usher	Deeds	n.d.	NAI M.3431 & D.20,447-53
Walker	see Gordon		

Family/Estate	Description	Timeframe	Reference
Walsh	Deeds and other papers	n.d.	NAI D.12,050 - 81, M.1057-63, T.3892-3903
Watson	see Finnegan		
Whelan	see Hackett		
White	97 deeds and some Wills	19th century	NAI D.7611-7707
Whittle	see Mullen		
Wide Street Commission	Deeds and maps,	c.1723-1844	NAI
Wilkinson	see Hayes and Shaw		
Wilson	Accounts	1844-1880	NLI Ms.5884
Wogan	see Clancy		
Woodcock	see Thomson		

Tenants Names	denominations
Alex.r Harpers rep.s	Mullinahack- City of Dublin
Mark Watson's rep.s	
Richard Powell	
Thos. Sharkey's rep.s	Bridge Street
John Brennans eep.s	
John Lee late Pentland	Back Lane
Rich.d Handcocks rep.s	Patrick Street
Thos. Archer	New Church Street
Mich.l McGanys Rep.s	
Thos. Costellows rep.s	
Cath.m Walkers rep.s	
Hugh Downeys Reps	Smithfield 7
d.t	d.t 8
Thos. Fallow late Downey	d.t 6
William Hanlons rep.s	
John Jameson	

from
Rental of estates of William Tighe in Dublin, 1826. NLI Ms. 872

131

THE PEMBERTONS OF DUBLIN

by Brian de Breffny

These lineages for several families of Pemberton associated with Dublin have been compiled from research in parish registers, the Registry of Deeds, civil registration, probate records, directories and newspapers. Miss Phillis K. Pemberton of Dublin kindly showed me her grandparents' family Bible, and Miss Elizabeth Kathleen Pemberton of Dublin and her sisters kindly provided a record of the descendants of their great-grandfather.

Pemberton of Dublin and of Mount Olive, Raheny, Co. Dublin

The birthplace, parentage and origins of Benjamin Pemberton, from whom this family descends, have not been discovered. By 1731 he was established in Dublin as a bricklayer and mason, but it is not known whether he was a native of the city or—as seems likely—one of the numerous men in the building trade who came to Ireland from England during the first quarter of the 18th century to participate in the then booming building industry (e.g. Elgee, see *The Irish Ancestor* 1972, and Wilde, see *The Irish Ancestor* 1973). It is of considerable interest that Benjamin's descendants in Dublin remained in the building industry for seven generations, right down to the present time, and for about 250 years have contributed to building in Dublin and its suburbs as bricklayers, masons, contractors, civil engineers and architects.

The earliest established ancestor in Ireland,

BENJAMIN PEMBERTON, bricklayer and mason, was of St Andrew's parish, Dublin, in 1731 and of Carter's Alley, parish of St Mark's, Dublin, in the 1740s. He m. 1stly (Prerog. MLB 16 Aug. 1731, which calls him a "cementer") Deborah, dau. of William Turner of Dublin, mason (Inventory Dublin Diocese 1741) by his wife Deborah (will proved Dublin 1742). On 27 Sept. 1731, apparently as a post-nuptial settlement, William Turner assigned a house in Carter's Alley, near Lazyhill, to his "son" Benjamin Pemberton. Deborah Pemberton was bur. at St Mark's 25 Feb. 1738, and Benjamin m. 2ndly (Prerog. MLB 31 Jan. 1740-1) Rachel Oliver of St Michan's parish, who was, bur. 11 June 1777 at St Mark's. According to tradition among her descendants in the 19th century she was of Huguenot extraction and owned a French Bible: her parentage has not been discovered although the will of her eldest son Benjamin in 1795 refers to his "grandfather Oliver." A Francois Olivier, cabinet-maker, and his wife Marie had children bapt. at the French Church, Peter St. and Lucy Lane, Dublin 1719-22; a Jean Olivier, stocking-maker, m. Madeleine Barré in the French Church of St Patrick, Dublin, 1699; the will of a John Oliver of Dublin, wigmaker, was proved 1732 (Prerog.), and the will of a Susanna Oliver of Dublin, widow, was proved 1758 (Prerog.). Benjamin was bur. at St Mark's 26 Aug. 1787; his will, dated. 16 May 1782 describes him as "of Dublin and Raheny," and was pd. 9 Jan. 1790 (Dublin). He had issue, all bapt. at St Mark's,

1. Deborah Mary, so bapt. 26 Feb. 1741 and so named in her MLB of 18 Feb. 1762, but erroneously entered as Rebecca in the register of her marriage; m. 19 Feb. 1762 (St Mark's) Stephen Rudd of St Anne's, Dublin, timber merchant, and had issue. He m. 2ndly 1772 Anne Jane Morris; his will, dat. 30 Aug. 1790 was pd. 18 Nov. 1790 (Prerog.).
2. Benjamin, of whom presently.

Family histories have been published in genealogy and local history journals. They have also been published as stand alone books.

Chapter 11   Family Names and Histories

Dublin City families are a mix of people from all parts of Ireland, and of immigrants. A large selection of histories and pedigrees have been published both independently and in the journals of local history and genealogical societies. These are very predominantly for the wealthier families. The private publications can be hard to locate, but the NLI or the local history section of the local library will generally have a copy. Sources for Irish Family History (Flyleaf Press, 2001 - www.flyleaf.ie/sources.htm) may also be useful.

Acton Papers (Stradbrook, Co. Dublin). Anal. Hib. 25: 3-13.
Arnoldi of Dublin, 27 Entries in Family Bible. JAPMD 8 (1910-12): 71.
Notes on the Cooke, *Ashe* and Swift Families, all of Dublin. J. Ass. Pres. Mem. Dead 9 (1912–16) 503.
***Ball** family records*. by Rev. Wm. Ball Wright. York: 1908.
*Some account of the family of **Barton*** by Bertram Francis Barton. Dublin: Cahill & Co. 1902
The Dublin Branch of the ***Barclays*** of Ury. In *The Barclays of New York ... and some other Barclays*. R. Burnham Moffat. Pub. R G Cooke, New York, 1904. Available at www.archive.org
Barnewall. Ir. Gen. 5 (2) (1975): 181-85.
The ***Barnewalls*** of Turvey. Reportorium 1 (2) (1956): 336-41.
*The **Barringtons** - a Family history*. Amy Barrington. Dublin 1917.
*The **Barringtons** of Glendruid* (Cabinteely, Co. Dublin). Moira Laffan. Foxrock Local History Club. Dublin: 1990.
The ***Bathes*** of Drumcondra. Reportorium 1 (2) (1956): 328-30.
Bellingham. In *'History of Santry and Clogher'*. B. J. Adams. London, 1883.
*The **Blackall** family of Limerick, Dublin and Clare* by Sir Henry Blackall, c. 1973
Castilla and the ***Bradstreet*** Family. Irish Family History 29 (2013) p. 90-95.
Bolton families in Ireland. Charles K. Bolton. Boston: Goodspeeds Bookshop Inc. 1937.
Brett family of Dublin, Meath, Sligo, Carlow. Information sought. Ir. Gen. Vol. 12 (12) 1957

The *Brocas* Family, Notable Dublin Artists. University Review 2 (6) (1959): 17-25: and Dublin Hist. Rec. XVII (1961/62) p 25-34.

The genealogy of James and Edmond *Byrne* of Dublin. JCKAS Vol. XIV (1) (1964-65) pp. 29-33

Burys in and out of Dublin. J. Gen. Soc. I. 2(1) (2001) 53-56.

Queries and some information on the genealogy of M. *Chamberlayne*, of Dublin and Gray's Inn, 1668; .. Ir.Gen. Vol. I (1) April, 1937

Cooke - See Ash

Butterhill and Beyond: an illustrated history of Cooper family of ..and Abbeville House, Co. Dublin. R. Austin Cooper. Pr.pr. Reading 1991 (ISBN 0951773607)

Corballis/Corbally families of Co. Dublin. Irish Family History Vol. VIII. 1992. pp. 84-93. The *Corbally* family of Co. Dublin. Dublin Hist. Rec. 46 (1) (1993) p.66.

The *Corballis* family of Nuttstown Co. Dublin Dublin Hist. Rec. Vol. 60 (2) 2007 171-189.

Capt. Francis *Cruise* (of Dublin) in 'King James' Irish Army List' (1689) Dublin, John D'Alton. (Notes on family members pre-1700)

Cusack Family of Meath and Dublin. Ir. Gen. 5 (3) (1976): 298-313; 5 (4) (1977): 464-70; 5 (5) (1978): 591-600; 5 (6) 1979: 673-84; 6 (2) (1981): 130-53; 6 (3) (1982): 285-98.

Dawson Street and the *Dawson* family. Dublin Hist. Rec. 17 (2) (1962) 62-73

Notes and Pedigrees of *Delafields* (De la Ffeld). NLI Pos. 9020.

Delanys of Delville. Dublin Hist. Rec. 9(4) (1948) 105-116

Denham of Dublin. C. H. Denham. Dublin, 1936.

Dix Family of Dublin, Entries from Family Bible. JAPMD 11 (1921-25): 490.

The *Dexters* of Dublin and Co. Kildare. Ir. Anc. 2 (1) (1970): 31-42.

John *Dongan* of Dublin - an Elizabethan gentleman and his family. by

Papers re the *Dowling* family of the Liberties, Dublin 1895-1937. NLI Ms 29,041

The *Duffy* publishing family. Ir.Gen, 13(4) 2013. Pp 426-435

Thos. P. *Dungan*. Baltimore: Gateway Press 1996.

The Rise and Fall of the *DuBedats* of Dublin. J. DLBHS 6 (1997) p 41-57.

Rathfarnham Castle: Adam Loftus and the *Ely* family. Pr.pr. nd.

A History of the *Eastwood* Family in Ireland, 1600-1850. JCLAHS Vol. 24, No. 3 (1999) pp. 407-430

Fagans of Feltrim. Reportorium 2 (1) (1958): 103-06.

The *Falkiners* of Abbotstown, Co. Dublin. JKAHS 8 (1915-17): 331-63.

Medical and Musical - the *Fannins* of Dublin. Dublin Hist. Rec. 49 (1) (1996) p.32-58.

Concerning the *Farran* family of Dublin. JAPMD 9 (4) 408

The *Fassbenders* and Dublin. David Fassbender. Dublin Pr.pr. 2009. NLI 10B 478

Fertullagh see Tyrrell.

Findlater - The Story of a Dublin Merchant Family 1774-2001. A & A Farmar 2001

The *Fitz Rerys*, Welsh Lords of Cloghran, Co. Dublin. J. Louth Arch. Soc. 5 (1921): 13-17.

The *Fitzwilliams* of Merrion. Reportorium 2 (1) 1958: 88-96.

The *Fogartys* of Kevin Street. J.Dun Laoghaire Gen. Soc. 6(3) 1997 pp 75-81.

Craobh de shliocht Chonaill: **Geoghegans** *of Dublin and Westmeath*. Joe MacEochagáin. Pub: Galway Pr.pr. 2005. NLI 9B 2603

Finding new *Gibney* Relatives. Irish Family History 27 (2011) pp 79-99.

The *Grehans* of Lehaunstown. J.Dun Laoghaire Gen. Soc. 6(2) 1997 pp 63-7

Notes on the Family of *Grierson* of Dublin. Ir. Gen. 2 (1953): 303-37.

Capt. Nicholas *Harold* in 'King James' Irish Army List' (1689) Dublin, John D'Alton.

Guinness see Magennis

The *Hickey* Family - Kingstown's Fenian Leaders. J. Dun Laoghaire Gen. Soc. 4(1) 1995. pp 25-28.

The *Hollywoods* of Artane. Reportorium 1 (2) 1956: 341-44.

Samuel *Hughes*, boot and shoe maker and farmer of Dublin. Irish Family History 16 (2000) 23

The Dublin family of *Jacob*. Dublin Hist.Rec. 2(4) (1940) 134-140; Irish families of Jacob of .. the city of Dublin. A. H. Jacob & J. H Glascott. Dublin Steam Printing Co. 1875

Kingsbury Pedigree in Swanzy Notebooks. RCB Library, Dublin.

Law Family. Pedigree. JAPMD 11 (1921-25): 444.

The *Lawless* Family. Reportorium 1 (2) (1956): 344-50.

Milltown Leesons; arch-rebels of the ascendancy. Ir.Gen. 4 (1968) 14–16.

The *Lockes* of Athgoe. Reportorium Novum 1 (1) (1955) 76–79

The *Magees* of Belfast and Dublin. Bigger, F. Belfast, 1916.

Pedigree of the Magennis (Guinness) family of New Zealand and of Dublin. Richard Linn. Christchurch, N.Z., 1897.

Moore of Rutland Square, Dublin. Swanzy Notebooks. RCB(L).

A *Moorhouse* Family of Dublin etc. Ir. Anc. 9 (1) (1977): 15-18.

Nottinghams of Ballyowen. Reportorium 1 (2) 1956: 323-24.

The *Parnell* family: Dublin Associations. Dublin Hist. Rec. XVI, (1960/61) p 86-95.

The *Parsons* of Monkstown, Birr and Newcastle upon Tyne. J.DLBHS 6 (1999) p.57-60.

Pemberton of Dublin. Ir. Anc. 11 (1) (1979): 14-26.

The *Plunketts* of Dunsoghly. Reportorium 1 (2) (1956): 330-36.

Plunketts of Portmarnock. Reportorium 2 (1) (1958): 106-08.

The *Putland* family of Dublin and Bray. Dublin Hist.Rec. Vol. 54 (2) (2001) 183-

An Early Dublin Candlemaker: History of the Family of *Rathborne*, Chandlers, Dublin. Dublin Hist. Record 14 (1957): 66-73.

Rooke papers 1699-1994 (collection of genealogical material). NLI.

The *Scurlocks* of Rathcredan. Reportorium 1 (1) (1955): 79-80.

Segraves of Cabra. Reportorium 1 (2) (1956): 324-28.

A Genealogical History of the Family of Sirr of Dublin. London, 1903.

Entries from Family Bible of Stirling *Smith* of Rush, Co. Dublin. Ir.Anc. 11(1) (1979) 3.

The Shaws of Terenure: a 19th century merchant family. Tony McCarthy. Four Courts Press (Dublin) 2010. ISBN 978 184682-262-9

A Stokes family of Dublin. A G Stokes. Melbourne 1986.

Swift - See Ash

Talbot de Malahide. Reportorium 2 (1) (1958): 96-103.

The *Talbots* of Belgard. Reportorium 1 (1) (1955): 80-83.

Genealogical Memoir of Family of *Talbot* of Malahide. 1829.

War and Peace - the Survival of the Talbots of Malahide 1641-71 by Joseph Byrne. Dublin: Irish Academic Press, 1997.

The Dublin Tweedys. 1650-1882 by Owen Tweedy. London, 1956.

Genealogical History of the Tyrrells of Castleknock, Co. Dublin. by J.H. Tyrrell. London, 1904.

The *Tyrrells* of Castleknock. R.S.A.I. 76 (1946): p.151-54.

Genealogical memoirs of the Ussher families in Ireland. By Rev. Wm. Ball Wright. Dublin: Sealy, Bryers & Walker. 1889.

Pedigree of *Verschoyle* of Donore, Co. Dublin, of City of Dublin, ... of Stillorgan Park, Co. Dublin, c.1690 -- 1891. NLI (GO): Ms.180, pp.301-9

Michael *Walsh*, merchant of Mt. Michael, Scholarstown. Co.Dublin. Irish Family History 22 (2006) 20

The Wildes of Merrion Square. Patrick Byrne. London and NY: Staples Press (1953)

Lineage of *Wolfe* of Leighon (Wolfe of Dublin). GO Ms. 543(3)

The *Woulfe* Flanagan family of Roscommon and Dublin. J. East Clare Heritage Group XI (1995) p. 110-118

The *Wolverstons* of Stillorgan. Reportorium 2 (2) (1960): p.243-45.

The Zlotover story by Hannah Berman and Dr M. Zlotover. Dublin, Hely Thom 1966.

Chapter 12

Further Reading and Miscellaneous Sources

There are many articles and books published on the history of specific townlands, parishes and villages, providing an interesting background to the place in which an ancestor lived. As some are published privately and some by local history societies they can be hard to locate. The researcher should first try the local history section or Irish section of their local library. The National Library of Ireland will generally hold a copy.

It is also worth trying 'Google Books' or https://archive.org/ to access copies of out of print titles. Some of these are free to download, usually in pdf format. Adobe Reader is required to open and view books downloaded in this format and is free to download from www.adobe.com or www.adobe.co.uk

Places

Artane	see **Coolock**
Ballybrack	see **Killiney**
Ballybough	Dowling and O'Reilly (Eds). *Mud Island, A History of Ballybough.* Dublin, Allen Library FAS Project 2002.
Ballymun	Somerville-Woodward, Robert. *Ballymun, A History. c.1600-1997* Synopsis (2 Vols.) Dublin 2002.
Balrothery	Hamilton, H.A. *History of the Parish of Balrothery.* Dublin, 1876.
Blackrock	MacCoil, Liam. *The Book of Blackrock.* Blackrock Council of Community Services. Carraig Books 1997.

Booterstown	Blacker, Rev. B.H. *Brief sketches of the Parishes of Booterstown and Donnybrook.* Geo. Herbert, Dublin 1874
	Knaggs, Robt. *Booterstown and Carysfort - a Parochial History 1821-1984.* Dublin 1984.
	Smyth, Hazel P. *The Town of the Road. The Story of Booterstown.* Pale Publishing 1994
Cabra	Neary, Bernard. *History of Cabra and Phibsboro,* Dublin: Raven Arts, 1984.
Carrickbrennan	English, Joe. *Carrickbrennan* Dun Laoghaire Borough Historical Society n.d.
Carrickmines	see **Tullow (Tully).**
Castleknock	O'Driscoll, James. *Cnucha - A history of Castleknock and District.* Dublin: 1977.
	Lacey, Jim. A *Candle in the Window, A History of the Barony of Castleknock.* Dublin, Mercier 2008.
Cloghran	Adams, Benjamin William. *History and Description of Santry and Cloghran Parishes.* London, Mitchell and Hughes 1883. see also **Mulhuddart**
Clondalkin	Ua Broin, Liam. *Clondalkin, Co. Dublin and its Neighbourhood.* RSAI 1944.
	Williams, Joe. *Clondalkin. Chronology and Historic Notes.* 1994.
Clontarf	McIntyre, Denis. *The Meadow of the Bull, A History of Clontarf.* Shara Press 1995.
Coolock	Appleyard, Douglas S. *Greenfields Gone Forever - the story of the Coolock and Artane Area.* Coolock Select Vestry: 1985.
Crumlin	see **Esker**
Dalkey	Edwards, B.L. *Dalkey.* Dublin: Jas. Duffy & Co. n.d.
	O'Flanagan, F.M. *Glimpses of Old Dalkey* Dublin Historical Record Vol.4 No.2 - p.41-57

	Kelly, M.R.L. *Dalkey, Co Dublin.* Arthur A. Stockwell Ltd. Ilfracombe 1952.
	Smith, Charles V. *Dalkey - Society and Economy in a small medieval Irish town.* IAP 1996.
	Wakeman, W F. *Antiquarian Notes on Dalkey, Killiney and Kill of the Grange.* Jnl. RSAI 1896.
Donabate	Brown, Rev. Robt. *Donabate Church - A short History.* Dublin 1940
Donnybrook	see **Booterstown**
Donnycarney	see **Fairview**
Dublin County	*Lewis' Dublin (1837), A Topographical Dictionary* Complied by Christopher Ryan Collins Press 2001
	D'Alton, John. *The History of the County of Dublin.* Dublin 1838.
	Ball, F.E. *History of County Dublin (6 vols.)* Dublin 1920. Reprint 1979.
Dublin City	McGregor, John James. *New Picture of Dublin, comprehending a History of the City.* Dublin 1821.
	Pearson, Peter. *The Heart of the City, Resurgence of an Historic City.* Dublin: O'Brien Press 2000.
	McCready, Rev. C.T. *Dublin Street Names ~ Dated and Explained* Dublin 1892, Carraig Books (1975).
	Clerkin, Paul *Dublin Street Names.* Gill and Macmillan 2001.
	Wright G.N. *An Historical Guide to the City of Dublin.* London 1825.
	Wakeman, W.F. *Dublin Delineated in Twenty Six Views of the Principal Public Buildings.* Dublin 1831. (Reprint: DCPL 2006) See p.54.
	Gilbert, John T. *A History of the City of Dublin.* Dublin and London 1861.

Dun Laoghaire (Kingstown)	Pearson, P. *Dun Laoghaire - Kingstown.* Dublin, O'Brien Press 1991.
	Pearson, P. *Between the Mountains and the Sea ~ Dun Laoghaire Rathdown County.* Dublin, O'Brien Press 2007.
	Historic Street Directory of Kingstown-Dun Laoghaire Dun Laoghaire Borough Historical Society 2000.
	O'Sullivan and Cannon (eds). *The Book of Dun Laoghaire.* Dublin: Blackrock Teachers Centre 1987.
	Callan, C. *Labour in Kingstown 1890-1920* Wicklow: 2016
Dundrum	Nolan, J. *The Changing Face of Dundrum.* Dublin: 1981. see also **Taney**
Esker	Curtis, Prof. Edmund. *The Court Book of Esker and Crumlin 1592-1600.* J.R.S.A.I. Series 6, Vol. XIX p.45-64 & 128-148, & Vol.XX p.38-55 & 137-149.
Fairview	Kingston, Rev. J. *The Parish of Fairview. including the present parishes of Corpus Christi, Glasnevin, Larkhill, Marino and Donnycarney.* Dundalgan Press 1953
Glasnevin	Egan, M.J. *The Story of Glasnevin.* Dublin, M.J. Egan 1963. see also Fairview
	Dublin Cemeteries Committee. *Prospect Cemetery Glasnevin* Dublin: 1904
Glasthule	Smith, Brian, *The Streets of Glasthule.* Dublin 2003
	Sweeney, Maxwell. *Parish by the Sea - the Story of St Joseph's, Glasthule 1869-1969.* Pub: Clergy of the Parish of St Joseph's, Dublin 1969
Grangegorman	Campbell, Rev. E.H.F. *100 years of life at Grangegorman 1828-1928.* Dublin 1928.

Inchicore	ÓBroin, Seosamh. *Inchicore, Kilmainham and District.* Cois Camóige Publications. n.d.
Irishtown	*see* **Sandymount**
Kilgobbin	Goodbody, Rob. *On the Borders of the Pale. (History of Kilgobbin, Stepaside and Sandyford).* Pale Publishing 1993.
Kill o' the Grange	Clare, Liam. *Kill of the Grange Pottery and Brick works.* Foxrock Local History Club 2003 -see also **Dalkey**
Killiney	Wakeman, W F. *Antiquarian notes on Dalkey, Killiney and Kill o' the Grange.* Jnl. RSAI 1896.
	Holy Trinity Church, Killiney (1858-1996) - A Parish History. Pub. by parish 1996.
	The Granite Hills, A Guide to Killiney and Ballybrack. Local History Group Ballybrack ICA Guild 1981. see also **Dalkey.**
Kilmainham	Kenny, C. *Kilmainham: the history of a settlement older than Dublin...* Blackrock: c.1995 see also **Inchicore**
Kiltiernan	O'Morchoe, Rev. Thomas A. *History of Kiltiernan and Kilgobbin.* Dublin: Church of Ireland 1934.
Kingstown	see **Dun Laoghaire**
Larkhill	see **Fairview**
Loughlinstown	Clarke, John Keogh. *History of Loughlinstown, County Dublin – Ancient, Modern and Extraneous.* n.d
Lucan	*The Manor of Lucan and the Restoration Land Settlement, 1660-1688.* Dublin Hist. Rec. 21 (1966-67): 139-43

Lusk	Monks, W. *Lusk - A Short History.* Old Fingal Society. 1978.
Marino	see **Fairview**
Merrion	Conroy, Colin . *Historic Merrion* Maidenswell Research Dublin 1996
Monkstown	Ball, F.E. *Some Residents of Monkstown in the 18th century.* J.R.S.A.I. Vol. IX (5th. Series) 1899.

Harden, Ralph W. *St John's Monkstown - the story of an Irish Parish.* Hodges Figgis, Dublin 1911.

Sweeney, Maxwell. *Monkstown: Story of a parish.* St Patrick's Parochial Committee, Monkstown 1966.

Stokes, Rev. A.E. *Where Monks Walked - The Story of Monkstown.* n.d. - see also **Seapoint**

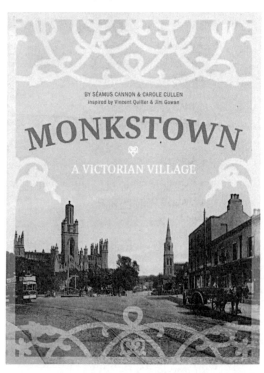

Monkstown - A Victorian Village by Séamus Cannon and Carole Cullen.
Blackrock Education Centre 2014

Mulhuddart	Ronan, Rev. Myles V. *Mulhuddart and Cloghran -Hiddert.* RSAI 1940.
Newcastle- Lyons	O'Sullivan, P. *Newcastle-Lyons: A Parish of the Pale.* Geography Publications, Dublin, 1985.
Palmerstown	O'Connor, Nessa. *Palmerstown - An Ancient Place.* 2007.
Phibsboro	see **Cabra**
Ranelagh	Kelly, Deirdre. *Four Roads to Dublin - History of Ranelagh, Rathmines and Leeson Street.* O'Brien Press 1995.
Rathdown	Pearson, P. *Between the Mountains and the Sea ~ Dun Laoghaire Rathdown County.* Dublin, O'Brien Press 2007.
Rathmichael	Turner, Kathleen. *Rathmichael - A Parish History.* Dublin: Select Vestry Rathmichael 1987.
Rathmines	see **Ranelagh**
Ringsend	Flynn, Arthur. *Ringsend and her Sister Villages.* Anna Livia Press 1990. *see also* **Sandymount**
Sallynoggin	Smith, Brian *The Streets of Sallynoggin.* Dun Laoghaire Jnl. No. 10 2001 p.32 – 40
Salthill	Scudds, Colin and Anna. *Salthill.* Dun Laoghaire Jnl. No.5 1996 p.44 - 48. see also **Seapoint**
Sandyford	see **Kilgobbin**
Sandymount	*The Roads to Sandymount, Irishtown, Ringsend.* - Sandymount Community Services 1996. *A Social and Natural history of Sandymount, Irishtown and Ringsend.* Sandymount Community Services 1993.
Seapoint	Tomas O'Rafferty, *The Seapoint and Salthill Story.* Monkstown. 1996.
Stepaside	see *Kilgobbin*

Stoneybatter	Kearns, Kevin C. *Stoneybatter, Dublin's Inner Urban Village.* Dublin, Gill and Macmillan, 1996.
Tallaght	Bagnall, Sean. *Tallaght 1835 - 1850, A Rural Place* Four Courts Press 2008.
	Handcock, William Domville. *The History and Antiquities of Tallaght in the County of Dublin.* Cork, Tower, 1976, c1899.
Taney	Ball, F.E. *The Parish of Taney: A History of Dundrum.* Hodges Figgis, Dublin 1895.
Tullow (Tully)	Simms, G.O. *Tullow's Story - a Portrait of a Co. Dublin Parish.* Dublin: Select Vestry of Tullow Parish, Carrickmines, 1983.
Whitechurch	Shepherd, E. *Behind the Scenes. The story of the Whitechurch District in South County Dublin.* Whitechurch Pubs. 1983.

General Reading

Ball, F.E. History of County Dublin. 6 vols. Dublin, 1920. Reprint. 1979.

Ball, F.E. An Historical Sketch of the Pembroke Township. Thom 1907.

Bennett, Douglas. Encyclopaedia of Dublin. Gill & Macmillan. 2005.

Brady, Karl. Shipwreck Inventory of Ireland - Louth, Meath, Dublin and Wicklow. Stationery Office Dublin 2008.

Carey, Tim. Dublin Since 1922. Hachette Books, 2016

Clark, Mary. Sources for Genealogical Research in Dublin Corporation Archives. Ir. Gen. 7(2) 1987, pp 291-2 .

Clark, Mary and Refausse, Raymond. Directory of Historic Dublin Guilds. Dublin Public Libraries, 1993.

Costello, Peter. Dublin Churches . Dublin 1989. ISBN 07171-1700 - 6.

Craig, Maurice. Dublin 1660 - 1860 - The Shaping of a City. Liberties Press, Dublin, 2006

Crawford, John. Within the Walls - the Story of St Audoen's Church, Cornmarket, Dublin. Dublin, 1986.

Crawford, John. Around the Churches - the Story of the churches in the St Patrick's Cathedral group of parishes, Dublin. Dublin, 1988.

Crawford, John. St. Catherine's Parish, Dublin 1840-1900 - A portrait of a Church of Ireland community. IAP 1996.

D'Alton, J. The History of Co. Dublin. Dublin, 1838. Reprint, Cork, Tower 1976.

DeCourcy, J W. The Liffey in Dublin Gill & Macmillan. 1996.

Donegan, William. S. Lucania - Topographical, Biographical and Historical. Dublin: Browne & Nolan 1902.

Fitzpatrick, Samuel A. Ossory. Dublin - Historical and Topographical Account of the City. (Reprint) Tower Books, Cork 1977.

Givens , John. A Guide to Dublin Bay: Mirror to the City. Liffey Press 2006. ISBN 1-905785-08-9

Harris, Walter. History and Antiquities of City of Dublin from earliest accounts. Dublin, 1776.

Hayden, Mary. Charity Children in 18th Century Dublin. Dublin. -Hist. Record Vol. V (3) 1943, p.92-107 & NLI Ms. 24,013

Henry, Brian Dublin Hanged - Crime, Law Enforcement and Punishment in Late 18th C. Dublin. Irish Academic Press 1994

Hood, Susan. Royal Roots - Republican Inheritance: The Survival of The Office of Arms. Woodfield Press. 2002. ISBN 0-9534293-3-4

Hynes, Daniel. Short History of Dublin. Cork: Killeen Books, 1996

Kilfeather, Siobhán. Dublin: A Cultural and Literary History. Dublin: Liffey Press, 2005. ISBN 1-904148-69-7

McCready,C.T. Dublin Street Names - Dated and explained. Dublin 1892.

McCullough, Niall. Dublin An Urban History: The Plan of the City. Lilliput Press 2007. ISBN: 978 1 84351 098 7

O'Donnell, E.E. The Annals of Dublin. Wolfhound Press 1987.

O'Dwyer, Frederick. Lost Dublin. Dublin: Gill & McMillan 1981.

Pearson, Peter. Between the Mountains and the Sea - Dun Laoghaire Rathdown County. O'Brien Press 2007.

Shannon, Denis. A History of the Parks of Dun Laoghaire Rathdown. Dun Laoghaire Rathdown County Council 2001.

Succession Lists of Parish Priests in Dublin Diocese 1771-1960. Dublin Hist. Rec. 3 (1) (1962): 178-90.

Warburton, J.W., Rev. J. Whitelaw, and Rev. R. Walsh. A History of the City of Dublin. From the earliest account to the present time; to which is added biographical notices of eminent men and copious appendices of its population, revenue, commerce and literature. London, Cadell, 1818.

Wood, Herbert (Ed.). Liberty of St. Sepulchre - 1586-1590: Court Book. RSAI, 1930.

Miscellaneous Sources

Ward-Perkins, Sarah. Select Guide to Trade Union Records in Dublin. Irish Manuscripts Commission 1996.

Directory of Graveyards in the Dublin Area - an Index and Guide to Burial Records in Dublin City and County. Dublin Public Libraries 1990; ISBN 0 0946841136.

The Industries of Dublin, Historical, Statistical and Biographical. An Account of leading businessmen, commercial interests, wealth and growth. London: Spencer & Blackett 1887/88.

Abstracts of the Acts of the Assembly of the City of Dublin from A.D. 1539 to A.D. 1752. Gilbert Library. Ms. 57-60

Charters and Documents of the Guild of the Holy Trinity or Merchant Guild of Dublin. A.D. 1438-1824. Gilbert Library Ms. 78-79

Charters and Documents of the Dublin Corporation of Cutlers, Painters, Stainers, and Stationers, also of the Dublin Guild of Bricklayers. Gilbert Library. Ms.81

Documents of the Guild of Tailors of Dublin. A.D. 1296-1753. Gilbert Library. M.80

Memorandum Rolls of the City of Dublin from 26 Henry VI. Gilbert Library. Ms. 54-55

Index to transcripts of Memorandum Rolls of the City of Dublin. A.D. 1447 to A.D. 1660. Gilbert Library. Ms. 56

Monday Books of the City of Dublin, A.D. 1567-1712. Gilbert Library. Ms. 44-45

Register of ye Mayors of Dublin. Gilbert Library. Ms.85

Transcript (A) of the Book of Charters belonging to the City of Dublin .. from 1667 ...to 1767. Gilbert Library. Ms.71-73

Gardiner's Dublin, A History and Topography of Mountjoy Square and Environs. National Council for Education Awards (1991)

Moravians of Dublin 1746-1980. Irish Roots 2 (1994) p 12.

The Huguenots in Dublin. Dublin Hist. Rec. 8 (1945-46): 110-34.

The Manor of Lucan and the Restoration Land Settlement, 1660-1688. Dublin Hist. Rec. 21 (1966-67): 139-43.

Rentals of the Earl of Shelburne's Estates (1755-76). Dub. Hist Record II (2) 1939 pp 55-58

McQuinn, Colm: Description of the holdings of Fingal County Council Archives. Dublin Hist. Rec. Vol. 60 (1) (2007) 106-110.

Royal College of Surgeons Roll of Licentiates. Name and address of graduating from RCSI 1785-1950. www.rcsi.ie/roll_of_licentiates

The Development of Ballybrack

in the Nineteenth Century

by Pól O Duibhir

(Read to the Old Dublin Society, 16th March, 1977)

1. TALLY HO

When the Civil Survey was taken in 1654[1] the land of Loughlins-town, including Ballybrack, was evenly divided between arable and pasture. Land use did not change very much during the early eighteenth century and around 1760 there was enough pasture to enable the Kilruddery Hunters to chase the fox from Bray Common to Cabinteely before finally driving him into the sea, probably somewhere off Vico Point. This exciting saga was put into verse by Thomas Mozeen and published to the tune Síle Ní Ghadhra.[2] The actor John O'Keeffe remembered ". . . a stag, at full speed with head and horns erect; and then a full pack of hounds in the regular order of pursuit; and after them the huntsman on his horse, winding his horn, followed up by a number of hunting squires, all on horseback, as I had often seen them near Dunleary and Bray, Laughlin's Town with Johnny Adair of Kiltiernan at their head".[3]

The Kilruddery song describes how, after the hunt, the hunters retired to the hospitality of the Earl of Meath at Kilruddery. No doubt on other similar occasions they stopped for some drink and revelry at the Inn in Loughlinstown owned by one of their number Owen Bray, referred to in the song as the Loughlinstown landlord. According to some, there was more going on in Owen Bray's than would have been publicly admitted at the time: "where neighbouring squires held their cock fights and carried on the grosser debaucheries that even they were ashamed to perpetrate in their own dwellings".[4] Mozeen, a frequent guest at the Inn wrote a song about Owen Bray's which gives us the incidental information that the Inn may well have been a stopping off place for visitors from England, heading south after a bumpy passage across the Irish sea.[5]

By 1814 when Anne Plumtre passed the way, Owen Bray's was no longer an Inn, but "a gentleman's seat". The house was too near the road for the gentleman's liking, however, so he moved the entrance to the back of the house, built a wall between it and the road and laid an avenue which comes out on to the main road some hundred yards towards Dublin.[6]

Although the area was beginning to become more a residential than an open hunting area at this stage, Lord Powerscourt's pack were still hunting in Ballybrack in 1815. It was on one of these

*The Dublin Historical Record has been publshed by
the Old Dublin Society since 1938.
The above exract of Ballybrack is from Vol. 31 (1) December 1977.*

Journals:

The Irish Genealogist *1937-*
Published by the IGRS. The first eight volumes (1937-1993) available at www.eneclann.ie. NLI: Ir 9291 i 2 and 1H 344 (from Vol.9 No.3 1996). Searchable index at www.irishancestors.ie

Dublin Historical Record *1938-*
Published by the Old Dublin Society. NLI: Ir 94133 d 23 (1938-1999) and 1H 257 (from Autumn 1999).

The Irish Ancestor *1969 - 1986*
A total of 37 issues and 4 supplements were published. The complete set is now available from www.eneclann.ie NLI: Ir 9205 i 3

The Pembertons of Dublin and Chicago - see page 136.

Journal of the Irish Family History Society *1985-*
Journal published annually by the Irish Family History Society.

Journal of the Genealogical Society of Ireland *1992-*
Formerly, as the Dun Laoghaire Genealogical Society, a quarterly journal was published from 1992 to 1999 NLI : Ir 9292 d 20, continuing thereafter as the Journal of the Genealogical Society of Ireland. NLI: 1H 343.

Gateway to the Past *1993 - 2006*
Journal published by the Ballinteer Family History Society. NLI: Ir 9292 b 69 and as the Journal of the Irish Family History Society, Ballinteer Branch NLI: Ir 9292 b

Chapter 13   Library, Archives and Society Addresses

Archive and Internet Information

As explained in the introduction, the records which you will need to access for your Dublin research are located in several different archives. Although many of these are now accessible on-line, some are still only available from these repositories. Below is a listing of the major archives (all of which have websites), and also other websites of value to your search.

Major Archives:

General Register Office (GRO).
www.groireland.ie
This is the central repository for birth, death and marriage records. Details of records available, costs, and access information on the website above. The headquarters is located in Roscommon (Tel: +353 (0) 90 6632900 LoCall: 1890 252076) however, a research facility is available in Dublin City in Werburgh Street.

National Archives of Ireland (NAI).
www.nationalarchives.ie
Bishop Street, Dublin 8. The NAI houses a vast collection of records generated by public bodies (censuses, wills, and government records etc). It also provides a professional genealogical advisory service. It is necessary to obtain a readers ticket to access the records, but this can be done on-site.

National Library of Ireland (NLI).
www.nli.ie
Kildare Street, Dublin 2. The holdings of the NLI are mainly those of non-government organisations or individuals (Books, estate papers, newspapers, etc.). It has a dedicated genealogical service and has made RC church records and other material available on-line. The Genealogical Office is part of the library.

Registry of Deeds.
www.landregistry.ie
Henrietta Street, Dublin 1. This archive holds deeds dating back to 1708. In the same building is the Land Registry, which has land records since 1892. Its website is a good introduction to the indexation and documentation on hand.

Valuation Office, Irish Life Centre.
www.valoff.ie
Abbey Street Lower, Dublin 1. This archive holds the valuation records of all Irish properties from 1846 as well as valuation maps from c. 1850 Its basis is the Griffith Valuation and changes in land occupancy for each holding can be tracked from its records.

Dublin City Library and Archive (DCLA).
www.dublincitypubliclibraries.ie.
138-144 Pearse Street, Dublin 2. Contains a wide variety of Dublin records, including those of Dublin Corporation for many centuries, and also donated material, books and newspapers.

Representative Church Body Library (RCB).
www.ireland.anglican.org/
Braemor Park, Churchtown, Dublin. The Library is the Church of Ireland's principal reference library and archives and manuscripts repository. Church of Ireland parish registers wills, deeds, maps, vestry records including registers of vestrymen, account books and preachers' books.

Military Archives.
www.militaryarchives.ie
Cathal Brugha Barracks, Rathmines, Dublin 6. Contains records of the Irish Defence Forces, including the Irish rebellion from 1913 – 1921.

Garda Archives (Police). *www.garda.ie/angarda/museum.html*
Contains much data, including documents and photographs, on police history going back before the establishing of the Irish Garda in 1922. Tel. (01) 6669998.

Society of Friends Historical Library (Quakers)
www.quakers-in-ireland.ie
Stocking Lane, Dublin 16

Major Websites:

The websites of the above archives are hugely valuable sources. In addition, there are other websites of value.

www.censusnationalarchives.ie   This site is run by the National Archives above and provides free access to the 1901 and 1911 census data.

http://registers.nli.ie/.   This site is run by the National Library and provides free access to Roman Catholic registers

www.askaboutireland.ie   Run by the Library Council of Ireland and largely aimed at schools, it provides access to Griffith Valuation, to many maps, and also downloads of local histories.

www.libraryireland.com   books and articles on Irish History, genealogy and culture.

www.irishgenealogy.ie   This government site is a portal to relevant websites, but also provides a free search and access to Irish Civil Registration records. A search facility for church records in parts of Dublin, Kerry, Carlow and Cork is also available.

www.presbyterianhistoryireland.com   The Belfast based library has an extensive collection of the records of Presbyterian congregations throughout Ireland.

http://methodisthistoryireland.org   the section on genealogy which gives information about Methodist chapels and congregations in Ireland.

www.irishjewishroots.com   Every person of the Jewish faith who every lived in Ireland has been documented Genealogist Stuart Rosenblatt.

www.rootsireland.ie   This is run by the Irish Family History Foundation (IFHF) and provides central access to a network of local county Heritage or genealogy centres with indexed church records. Initial search is free, but a fee is charged for access to the details.

www.findmypast.ie   This site provides subscription-based access to many records including Prison records; Petty Sessions court; and a range of directories, military sources etc.

http://sources.nli.ie   A database of sources of Irish relevance in archives in Ireland and elsewhere. It is worth a search for your area interest.

http://databases.dublincity.ie This website is a portal to a series of databases maintained by Dublin City Council, including graveyards, directories, electoral lists etc.

www.logainm.ie/en A place names database, with a list of available sources for each townland

www.irishnewsarchive.com A subscription-based digital archive of Irish newspapers

www.irishtimes.com/archive A digital archive of the Irish Times dating back to 1859

In addition to the above specialist Irish sites, other international websites (*Ancestry.com; familysearch.org* etc.) will also contain many Irish records.

Societies and Sources:

Irish Genealogical Research Society. http://www.irishancestors.ie. Individual member-based Society which publishes the Irish Genealogist and also has several valuable on-line resources available to members.

Genealogical Society of Ireland www.familyhistory.ie. Individual member-based Society which publishes the Genealogical Society of Ireland journal.

Irish Family History Society www.ifhs.ie Also accepts members and publishes an annual journal and news-sheets.

Irish Roots Magazine www.irishrootsmagazine.com. A quarterly magazine dedicated to Irish genealogy

Swords Historical Society www.swordsheritage.com hold a range of genealogical transcripts and indexes for the Fingal area of Dublin. They are based at the Carnegie Library, North Street, Swords, Co. Dublin.

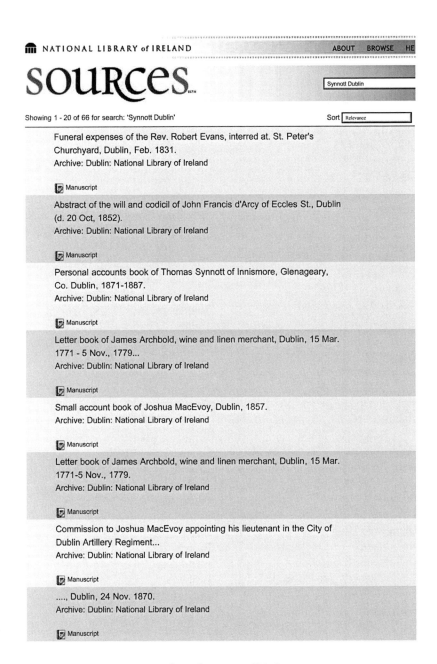

ABOUT   BROWSE   HE

SOURCES.

Synnott Dublin

Showing 1 - 20 of 66 for search: 'Synnott Dublin'   Sort | Relevance

Funeral expenses of the Rev. Robert Evans, interred at. St. Peter's
Churchyard, Dublin, Feb. 1831.
Archive: Dublin: National Library of Ireland

Manuscript

Abstract of the will and codicil of John Francis d'Arcy of Eccles St., Dublin
(d. 20 Oct, 1852).
Archive: Dublin: National Library of Ireland

Manuscript

Personal accounts book of Thomas Synnott of Innismore, Glenageary,
Co. Dublin, 1871-1887.
Archive: Dublin: National Library of Ireland

Manuscript

Letter book of James Archbold, wine and linen merchant, Dublin, 15 Mar.
1771 - 5 Nov., 1779...
Archive: Dublin: National Library of Ireland

Manuscript

Small account book of Joshua MacEvoy, Dublin, 1857.
Archive: Dublin: National Library of Ireland

Manuscript

Letter book of James Archbold, wine and linen merchant, Dublin, 15 Mar.
1771-5 Nov., 1779.
Archive: Dublin: National Library of Ireland

Manuscript

Commission to Joshua MacEvoy appointing his lieutenant in the City of
Dublin Artillery Regiment...
Archive: Dublin: National Library of Ireland

Manuscript

...., Dublin, 24 Nov. 1870.
Archive: Dublin: National Library of Ireland

Manuscript

http://sources.nli.ie/
is the National Library of Ireland database for Irish research,
containing over 180,000 catalogue records for Irish manuscripts
and for articles in Irish periodicals.

Index